BLACK&DECKER® HERE'S HOW...

PLUMBING

22 Easy Fix It Repairs to Save You Money & Time

Creative Publishing
international

MINNEAPOLIS, MINNESOTA
www.creativepub.com

Contents

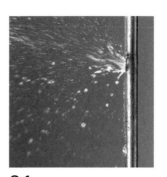

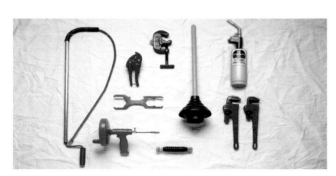

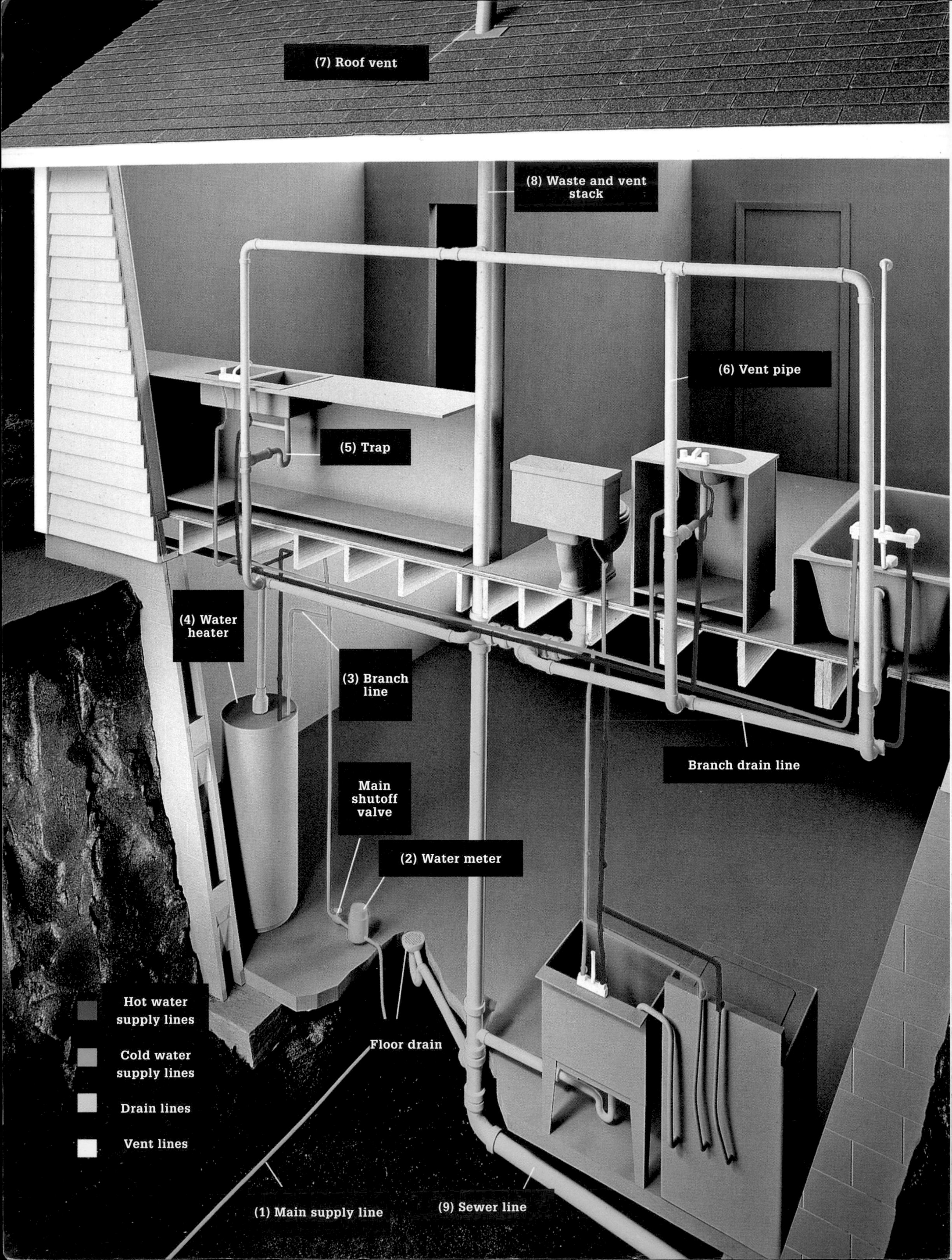

(7) Roof vent

(8) Waste and vent stack

(6) Vent pipe

(5) Trap

(4) Water heater

(3) Branch line

Main shutoff valve

(2) Water meter

Branch drain line

Hot water supply lines

Cold water supply lines

Drain lines

Vent lines

Floor drain

(1) Main supply line

(9) Sewer line

Introduction

For bargain-conscious homeowners, *Here's How: Plumbing* offers complete information on the 22 critical plumbing projects that do-it-yourselfers are likely to face.

Unlike larger, more expensive volumes this book doesn't include the background information on plumbing systems. Nor does it include exhaustive information on working with various plumbing materials. And it also leaves out a few projects that are of more interest to professional plumbers and contractors than to homeowners.

But *Here's How: Plumbing* does give you all the information you need to effectively deal with all the most common home plumbing problems that are likely to arise. If you see yourself as a novice or even intermeditate DIYer, this may well be the only book you'll need.

With *Here's How: Plumbing*, you'll be able to diagnose and fix a leaky faucet anywhere in your home; and if you no longer want to fix the faucet, you'll be able to replace it. You'll also learn how to clear all manner of clogged drains, from basement floor drains to bathroom toilets, sinks and tubs. Some key emergency repairs, such as patching a burst pipe, are also included.

Replacing an old toilet or vanity? No problem, with *Here's How: Plumbing*. Install a tub-shower surround, or a sliding shower door? Here's your book.

Replace a kitchen sink? Check.

Installing shut off valves? Check.

A helpful appendix at the end of the book shows the common plumbing tools you may find useful in making all these plumbing repairs, and more.

Today, a professional plumber often charges $100 per hour or more to come to your home to make repairs you can easily do yourself in a few minutes. Is there anybody who really wants to waste that kind of money? Armed with this low-cost book, you'll easily save hundreds of dollars a year by doing the work yourself.

1. Fixing Leaky Sink Faucets

It's not surprising that sink faucets leak and drip. Any fitting that contains moving mechanical parts is susceptible to failure. But add to the equation the persistent force of water pressure working against the parts, and the real surprise is that faucets don't fail more quickly or often. It would be a bit unfair to say that the inner workings of a faucet are regarded as disposable by manufacturers, but it is safe to say that these parts have become more easy to remove and replace.

The most important aspect of sink faucet repair is identifying which type of faucet you own. In this chapter we show all of the common types and provide instructions on repairing them. In every case, the easiest and most reliable repair method is to purchase a replacement kit with brand new internal working parts for the model and brand of faucet you own.

Tools & Materials ▶

Pliers	Repair kit
Needlenose pliers	(exact type varies)
Heatproof grease	Teflon tape
Channel-type pliers	Screwdrivers
Utility knife	Pipe joint compound
White Vinager	Plumber's putty
Old toothbrush	Rag
Tape measure	

Eventually, just about every faucet develops leaks and drips. Repairs can usually be accomplished simply by replacing the mechanical parts inside the faucet body (the main trick is figuring out which kind of parts your faucet has).

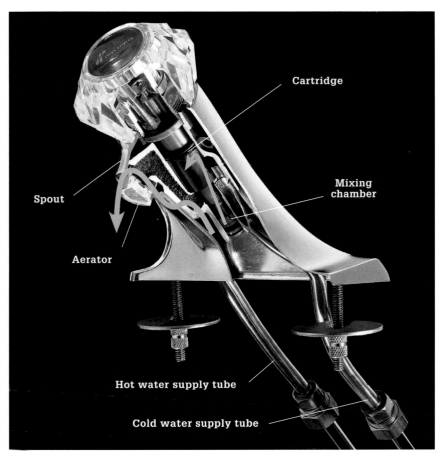

Almost all leaks are caused by malfunctioning faucet valve mechanisms. Whether your sink faucet is a one-handle cartridge type (left) or a two-handle compression type or anything in between, the solution to fixing the leak is to clean or replace the parts that seal off the hot and cold water inlets from the spout.

Cartridge

Spout

Mixing chamber

Aerator

Hot water supply tube

Cold water supply tube

Common Problems and Repairs ▶

Problems	Repairs
Faucet drips from the end of the spout or leaks around the base.	1. Identify the faucet design (page 8), then install replacement parts, using directions on the following pages.
Old worn-out faucet continues to leak after repairs are made.	1. Replace the old faucet (page 28).
Water pressure at spout seems low, or water flow is partially blocked.	1. Clean faucet aerator (page 14). 2. Replace corroded galvanized pipes with copper.
Water pressure from sprayer seems low, or sprayer leaks from handle.	1. Clean sprayer head (page 14). 2. Fix diverter valve (page 23).
Water leaks onto floor underneath faucet.	1. Replace cracked sprayer hose. 2. Tighten water connections, or replace supply tubes and shutoff valves. 3. Fix leaky sink strainer.
Hose bib or valve drips from spout or leaks around handle.	1. Take valve apart and replace washers and O-rings.

Common Faucet Types

A leaky faucet is the most common home plumbing problem. Leaks occur when washers, O-rings, or seals inside the faucet are dirty or worn. Fixing leaks is easy, but the techniques for making repairs will vary, depending on the design of the faucet. Before beginning work, you must first identify your faucet design and determine what replacement parts are needed.

There are four basic faucet designs: ball-type, cartridge, disc, and compression. Many faucets can be identified easily by outer appearance, but others must be taken apart before the design can be recognized.

The compression design is used in many double-handle faucets. Compression faucets all have washers or seals that must be replaced from time to time. These repairs are easy to make, and replacement parts are inexpensive.

Ball-type, cartridge, and disc faucets are all known as washerless faucets. Many washerless faucets are controlled with a single handle, although some cartridge models use two handles. Washerless faucets are more trouble-free than compression faucets and are designed for quick repair.

When installing new faucet parts, make sure the replacements match the original parts. Replacement parts for popular washerless faucets are identified by brand name and model number. To ensure a correct selection, you may want to bring the worn parts to the store for comparison.

Ball-type faucet has a single handle over a dome-shaped cap. If your single-handle faucet is made by Delta® or Peerless®, it is probably a ball-type faucet. See page 12 to fix a ball-type faucet.

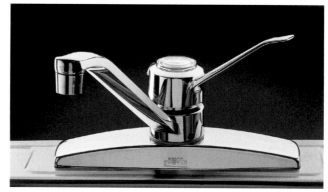

Cartridge faucets are available in single-handle or double-handle models. Popular cartridge faucet brands include Price Pfister™, Moen, Valley, and Aqualine. See page 11 to fix a cartridge faucet.

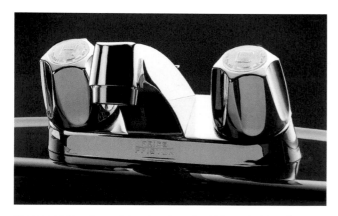

Compression faucet has two handles. When shutting the faucet off, you usually can feel a rubber washer being squeezed inside the faucet. Compression faucets are sold under many brand names. See page 10 to fix a compression faucet.

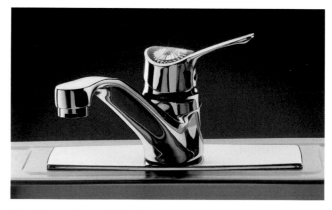

Disc faucet has a single handle and a solid, chromed-brass body. If your faucet is made by American Standard or Reliant, it may be a disc faucet. See page 13 to fix a disc faucet.

Faucet Repair Kits

Repair kit for a ball-type faucet includes rubber valve seats, springs, cam, cam washer, and spout O-rings. Kit may also include small Allen wrench tool used to remove faucet handle. Make sure kit is made for your faucet model. Replacement ball can be purchased separately but is not needed unless old ball is obviously worn.

Replacement cartridges come in dozens of styles. Cartridges are available for popular faucet brands, including (from left) PricePfister™, Moen, and Kohler. O-ring kits may be sold separately.

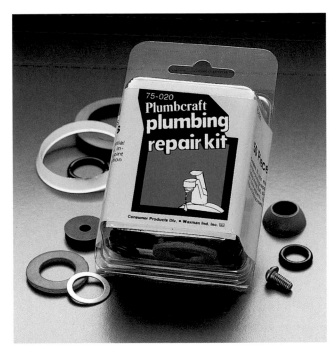

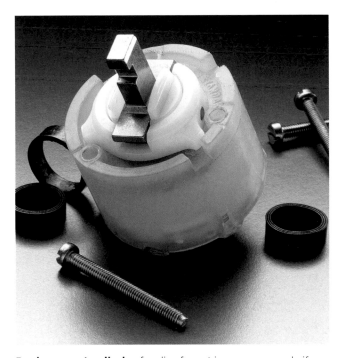

Universal washer kit contains parts needed to fix most types of compression faucets. Choose a kit that has an assortment of neoprene washers, O-rings, packing washers, and brass stem screws.

Replacement cylinder for disc faucet is necessary only if faucet continues to leak after cleaning. Continuous leaking is caused by cracked or scratched ceramic discs. Replacement cylinders come with neoprene seals and mounting screws.

Compression Faucets

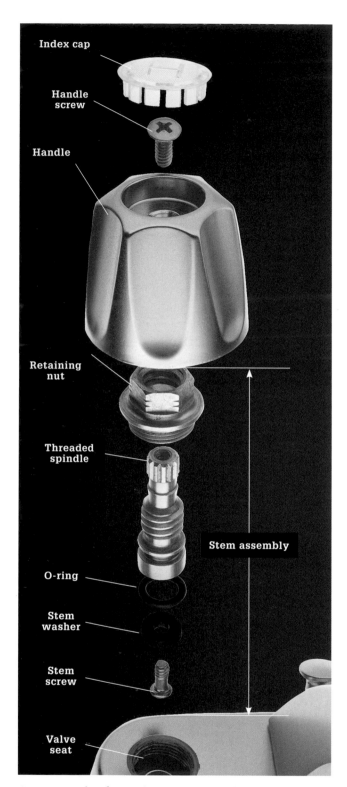

Index cap

Handle screw

Handle

Retaining nut

Threaded spindle

Stem assembly

O-ring

Stem washer

Stem screw

Valve seat

Stem assembly

Faucet body

Remove the faucet handles so you can grasp the retaining nut for the stem assembly with pliers. Loosen the nut and remove the entire stem assembly.

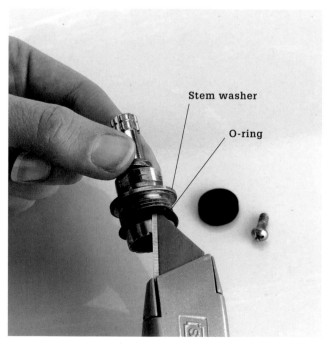

Stem washer

O-ring

A compression faucet has a stem assembly that includes a retaining nut, threaded spindle, O-ring, stem washer, and stem screw. Dripping at the spout occurs when the washer becomes worn. Leaks around the handle are caused by a worn O-ring.

Remove the old O-ring and replace it with a new one. Also replace the stem washer. Clean all parts with white vinegar, scrubbing with an old toothbrush if necessary. Coat the new O-ring and stem washer with heatproof grease and reassemble the valve.

Cartridge Faucets

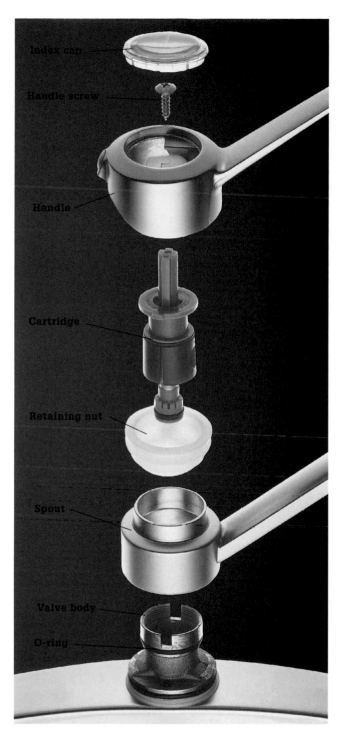

- Index cap
- Handle screw
- Handle
- Cartridge
- Retaining nut
- Spout
- Valve body
- O-ring

Retaining nut

Remove the faucet handle and withdraw the old cartridge. Make a note of how the cartridge is oriented before you remove it. Purchase a replacement cartridge.

Install the replacement cartridge. Clean the valve seat first and coat the valve seat and O-rings with heatproof grease. Be sure the new cartridge is in the correct position, with its tabs seated in the slotted body of the faucet. Re-assemble the valve and handles.

Both one- and two-handle faucets are available with replaceable plastic cartridges inside the faucet body. These cartridges (used by PricePfister™, Sterling, Kohler, Moen, and others) regulate the flow of water through the spout, and in single-handle faucets they also mix the hot and cold water to alter the temperature out of the spout. To locate the correct replacement cartridge for your faucet, knowing the manufacturer and model number is a great help.

Ball Faucets

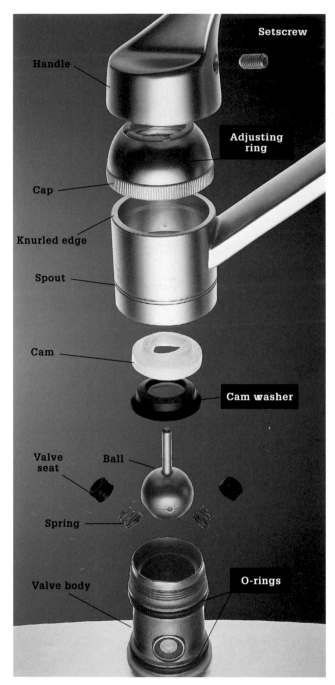

Handle

Setscrew

Adjusting
ring

Cap

Knurled edge

Spout

Cam

Cam washer

Valve
seat

Ball

Spring

Valve body

O-rings

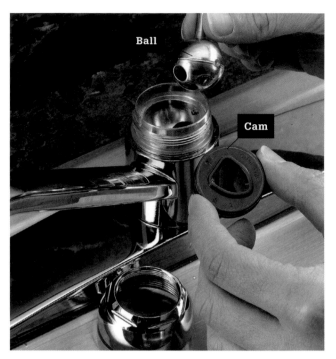

Ball

Cam

Remove the old ball and cam after removing the faucet handle and ball cap. Some faucets may require a ball faucet tool to remove the handle. Otherwise, simply use a pair of channel-type pliers to twist off the ball cap.

The ball-type faucet is used by Delta, Peerless, and a few others. The ball fits into the faucet body and is constructed with three holes (not visible here)—a hot inlet, a cold inlet, and the outlet, which fills the valve body with water that then flows to the spout or sprayer. Depending on the position of the ball, each inlet hole is open, closed, or somewhere in-between. The inlet holes are sealed to the ball with valve seats, which are pressed tight against the ball with springs. If water drips from the spout, replace the seats and springs. Or go ahead and purchase an entire replacement kit and replace all or most of the working parts.

Pry out the neoprene valve seals and springs and replace them with new parts. Also replace the O-rings on the valve body. You may want to replace the ball and cam, too, especially if you're purchasing a repair kit. Coat all rubber parts in heatproof grease, and reassemble the faucet.

Disc Faucets

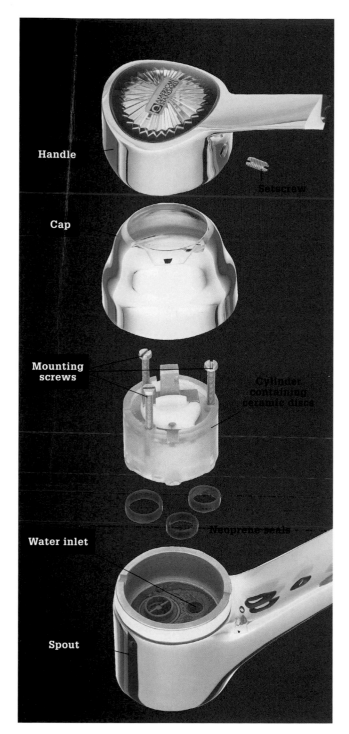

Handle

Setscrew

Cap

Mounting screws

Cylinder containing ceramic discs

Water inlet

Neoprene seals

Spout

The disc-type faucet used by American Standard, among others, has a wide disc cartridge hidden beneath the handle and the cap. Mounting screws hold the cartridge in the valve body. Two tight-fitting ceramic discs with holes in them are concealed inside the cartridge. The handle slides the top disc back and forth and from side to side over the stationary bottom disc. This brings the holes in the disks into and out of alignment, adjusting the flow and mix of hot and cold water.

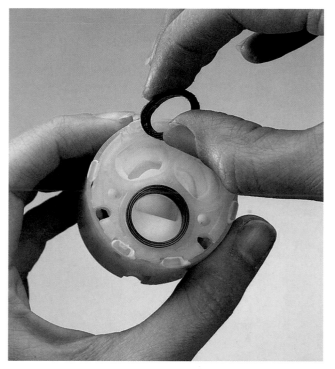

Disassemble the faucet handle and remove the old disc. You'll need to unscrew the three long mounting screws all the way to get the cylinder containing the ceramic discs out of the faucet.

Replace the cylinder with a new one, coating the rubber parts with heatproof grease before installing the new cylinder. Make sure the rubber seals fit correctly in the cylinder openings before you install the cylinder. Assemble the faucet handle.

2. Repairing Sprayers & Aerators

If water pressure from a sink sprayer seems low, or if water leaks from the handle, it is usually because lime buildup and sediment have blocked small openings inside the sprayer head. To fix the problem, first take the sprayer head apart and clean the parts. If cleaning the sprayer head does not help, the problem may be caused by a faulty diverter valve. The diverter valve inside the faucet body shifts water flow from the faucet spout to the sprayer when the sprayer handle is pressed. Cleaning or replacing the diverter valve may fix water pressure problems.

Whenever making repairs to a sink sprayer, check the sprayer hose for kinks or cracks. A damaged hose should be replaced.

If water pressure from a faucet spout seems low, or if the flow is partially blocked, take the spout aerator apart and clean the parts. The aerator is a screw-on attachment with a small wire screen that mixes tiny air bubbles into the water flow. Make sure the wire screen is not clogged with sediment and lime buildup. If water pressure is low throughout the house, it may be because galvanized iron water pipes are corroded.

Tools & Materials ›

Screwdriver
Channel-type pliers
Needlenose pliers
Small brush
Vinegar

Universal washer kit
Heatproof grease
Replacement
   sprayer hose

Kitchen sprayers are very convenient and, in theory, quite simple. Yet, they break down with surprising regularity. Fixing or replacing one is an easy job, however.

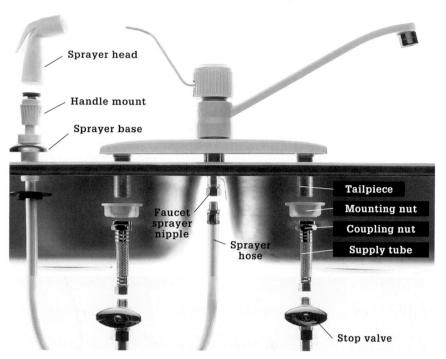

Sprayer head

Handle mount

Sprayer base

Faucet sprayer nipple

Sprayer hose

Tailpiece

Mounting nut

Coupling nut

Supply tube

Stop valve

The standard sprayer hose attachment is connected to a nipple at the bottom of the faucet valve. When the lever of the sprayer is depressed, water flows from a diverter valve in the faucet body out to the sprayer. If your sprayer stream is weak or doesn't work at all, the chances are good that the problem lies in the diverter valve.

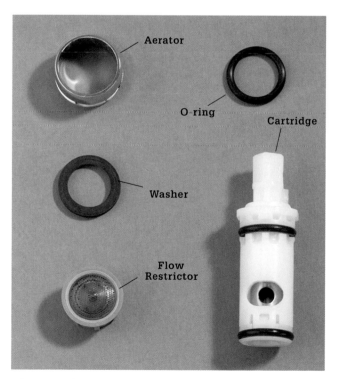

Aerator

O-ring

Cartridge

Washer

Flow Restrictor

Diverter valves and aerators differ from faucet to faucet, so you'll need to know the make and model if your faucet to purchase replacement. However, if you bring the old parts in to the plumbing supply store, they can probably find the right replacements for you.

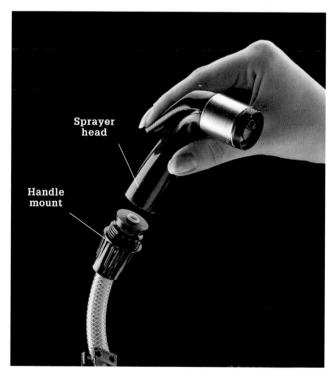

Sprayer head

Handle mount

Sprayer heads can be removed from the sprayer hose, usually by loosening a retaining nut. By removing the head, disassembling it as much as you can and cleaning it you may be able to solve a weak spray problem.

How to Repair a Sprayer

Shut off the water at the stop valves and remove the faucet handle to gain access to the faucet parts. Disassemble the faucet handle and body to expose the diverter valve. Ball-type faucets like the one shown here require that you also remove the spout to get at the diverter.

Locate the diverter valve, seen here at the base of the valve body. Because different types and brands of faucets have differently configured diverters, do a little investigating beforehand to try and locate information about your faucet. The above faucet is a ball type.

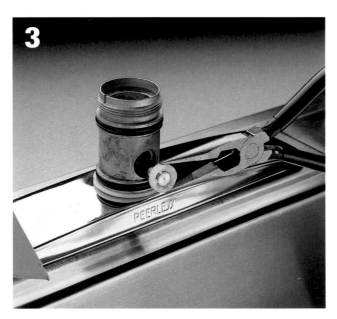

Pull the diverter valve from the faucet body with needlenose pliers. Use a toothbrush dipped in white vinegar to clean any lime buildup from the valve. If the valve is in poor condition, bring it to the hardware store and purchase a replacement.

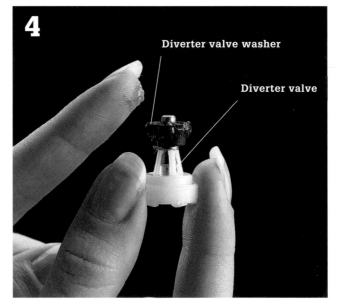

Coat the washer or O-ring on the new or cleaned diverter valve with heatproof grease. Insert the diverter valve back into the faucet body. Reassemble the faucet. Turn on the water and test the sprayer. If it still isn't functioning to your satisfaction, remove the sprayer tip and run the sprayer without the filter and aerator in case any debris has made its way into the sprayer line during repairs.

How to Repair a Kitchen Sprayer

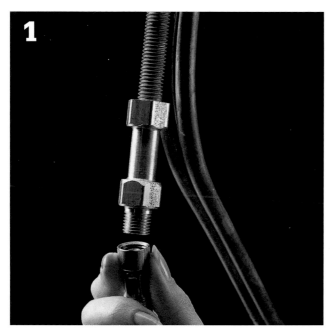

To replace a sprayer hose, start by shutting off the water at the shutoff valves. Clear out the cabinet under your sink and put on eye protection. Unthread the coupling nut that attaches the old hose to a nipple or tube below the faucet spout. Use a basin wrench if you can't get your channel-type pliers on the nut.

Unscrew the mounting nut of the old sprayer from below and remove the old sprayer body. Clean the sink deck and then apply plumber's putty to the base of the new sprayer. Insert the new sprayer tailpiece into the opening in the sink deck.

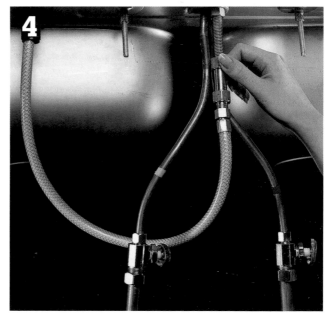

From below, slip the friction washer up over the sprayer tailpiece. Screw the mounting nut onto the tailpiece and tighten with a basin wrench or channel-type pliers. Do not overtighten. Wipe away any excess plumber's putty.

Screw the coupling for the sprayer hose onto the hose nipple underneath the faucet body. For a good seal, apply pipe joint compound to the nipple threads first. Tighten the coupling with a basin wrench, turn on the water supply at the shutoff valves, and test the new sprayer.

3. Fixing & Replacing Showerheads

If spray from the showerhead is uneven, clean the spray holes. The outlet or inlet holes of the showerhead may get clogged with mineral deposits. Showerheads pivot into different positions. If a showerhead does not stay in position, or if it leaks, replace the O-ring that seals against the swivel ball.

A tub can be equipped with a shower by installing a flexible shower adapter kit. Complete kits are available at hardware stores and home centers.

Tools & Materials ▶

Adjustable wrench
    or channel-type
    pliers
Pipe wrench
Drill
Glass and tile bit
Mallet
Screwdriver

Masking tape
Thin wire (paper clip)
Heatproof grease
Rag
Replacement O-rings
Masonry anchors
Flexible shower adapter
    kit (optional)

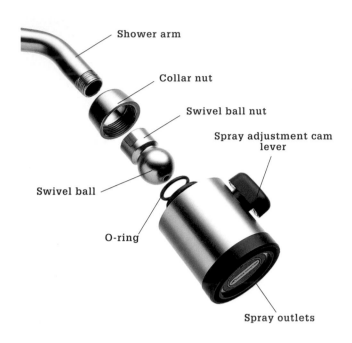

A typical showerhead can be disassembled easily for cleaning and repair. Some showerheads include a spray adjustment cam lever that is used to change the force of the spray.

How to Clean & Repair a Showerhead

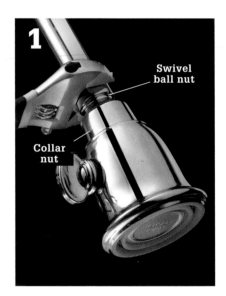

Unscrew the swivel ball nut, using an adjustable wrench or channel-type pliers. Wrap jaws of the tool with masking tape to prevent marring the finish. Unscrew collar nut from the showerhead.

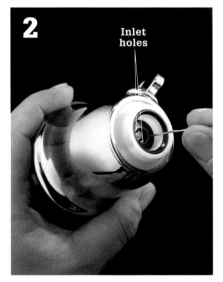

Clean outlet and inlet holes of showerhead with a thin wire. Flush the head with clean water.

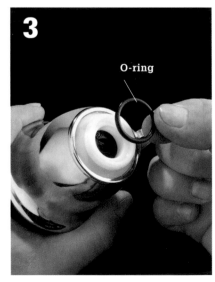

Replace the O-ring, if necessary. Lubricate the O-ring with heatproof grease before installing.

How to Install a Flexible Shower Adapter

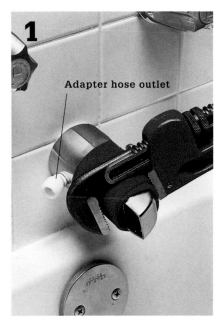

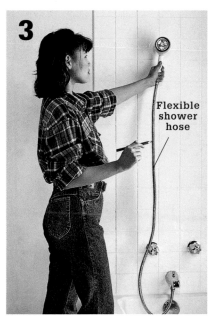

Remove old tub spout. Install new tub spout from kit, using a pipe wrench. New spout will have an adapter hose outlet. Wrap the tub spout with a rag to prevent damage to the chrome finish.

Attach flexible shower hose to the adaptor hose outlet. Tighten with an adjustable wrench or channel-type pliers.

Determine location of showerhead hanger. Use hose length as a guide, and make sure shower-head can be easily lifted off hanger.

Mark hole locations. Use a glass and tile bit to drill holes in ceramic tile for masonry anchors.

Insert anchors into holes, and tap into place with a wooden or rubber mallet.

Fasten showerhead holder to the wall, and hang showerhead.

4. Fixing Tub & Shower Faucets

Tub and shower faucets have the same basic designs as sink faucets, and the techniques for repairing leaks are the same as described in the faucet repair section of this book (pages 6 to 13). To identify your faucet design, you may have to take off the handle and disassemble the faucet.

When a tub and shower are combined, the showerhead and the tub spout share the same hot and cold water supply lines and handles. Combination faucets are available as three-handle, two-handle, or single-handle types (next page). The number of handles gives clues as to the design of the faucets and the kinds of repairs that may be necessary.

With combination faucets, a diverter valve or gate diverter is used to direct water flow to the tub spout or the showerhead. On three-handle faucet types, the middle handle controls a diverter valve. If water does not shift easily from tub to showerhead, or if water continues to run out the spout when the shower is on, the diverter valve probably needs to be cleaned and repaired (page 23).

Two-handle and single-handle types use a gate diverter that is operated by a pull lever or knob on the tub spout. Although gate diverters rarely need repair, the lever occasionally may break, come loose, or refuse to stay in the up position. To repair a gate diverter set in a tub spout, replace the entire spout.

Tub and shower faucets and diverter valves may be set inside wall cavities. Removing them may require a deep-set ratchet wrench.

If spray from the showerhead is uneven, clean the spray holes. If the showerhead does not stay in an upright position, remove the head and replace the O-ring.

To add a shower to an existing tub, install a flexible shower adapter. Several manufacturers make complete conversion kits that allow a shower to be installed in less than one hour.

Tub/shower plumbing is notorious for developing drips from the tub spout and the showerhead. In most cases, the leak can be traced to the valves controlled by the faucet handles.

Tub & Shower Combination Faucets

Three-handle faucet (page 22) has valves that are either compression or cartridge design.

Two-handle faucet (page 24) has valves that are either compression or cartridge design.

Single-handle faucet (page 26) has valves that are cartridge, ball-type, or disc design.

Fixing Three-handle Tub & Shower Faucets

A three-handle faucet type has two handles to control hot and cold water, and a third handle to control the diverter valve and direct water to either a tub spout or a shower head. The separate hot and cold handles indicate cartridge or compression faucet designs.

If a diverter valve sticks, if water flow is weak, or if water runs out of the tub spout when the flow is directed to the showerhead, the diverter needs to be repaired or replaced. Most diverter valves are similar to either compression or cartridge faucet valves. Compression-type diverters can be repaired, but cartridge types should be replaced.

Remember to turn off the water before beginning work.

Tools & Materials ▶

Screwdriver
Adjustable wrench
  or channel-type
  pliers
Deep-set
  ratchet wrench
Small wire brush

Replacement
  diverter cartridge
  or universal
  washer kit
Heatproof grease
Vinegar

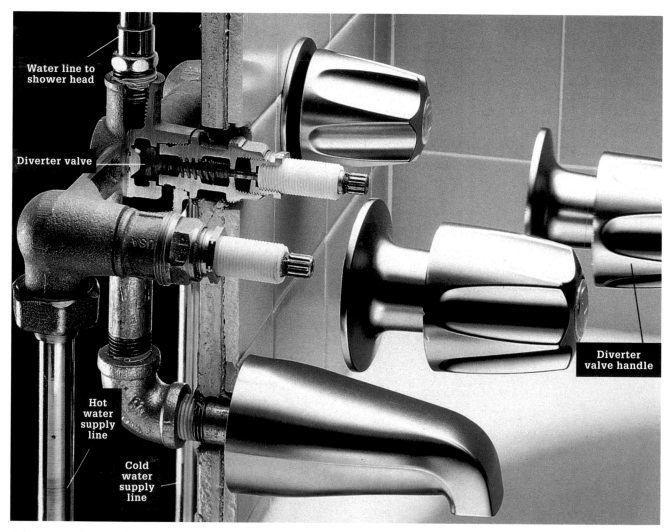

A three-handle tub/shower faucet has individual controls for hot and cold water plus a third handle that operates the diverter valve.

How to Repair a Compression Diverter Valve

Remove the diverter valve handle with a screwdriver. Unscrew or pry off the escutcheon.

Remove bonnet nut with an adjustable wrench or channel-type pliers.

Unscrew the stem assembly, using a deep-set ratchet wrench. If necessary, chip away any mortar surrounding the bonnet nut.

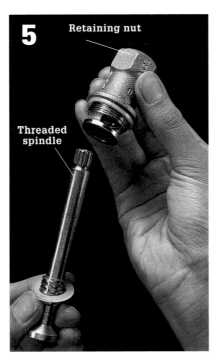

Remove brass stem screw. Replace stem washer with an exact duplicate. If stem screw is worn, replace it.

Unscrew the threaded spindle from the retaining nut.

Clean sediment and lime buildup from nut, using a small wire brush dipped in vinegar. Coat all parts with heatproof grease, and reassemble diverter valve.

Fixing Two-handle Tub & Shower Faucets

Two-handle tub and shower faucets are either cartridge or compression design. They may be repaired following the directions on pages 23 and 27. Because the valves of two-handle tub and shower faucets may be set inside the wall cavity, a deep-set socket wrench may be required to remove the valve stem.

Two-handle tub and shower designs have a gate diverter. A gate diverter is a simple mechanism located in the tub spout. A gate diverter closes the supply of water to the tub spout and redirects the flow to the shower head. Gate diverters seldom need repair. Occasionally, the lever may break, come loose, or refuse to stay in the up position.

If the diverter fails to work properly, replace the tub spout. Tub spouts are inexpensive and easy to replace.

Remember to turn off the water before beginning any work.

Tools & Materials ▸

Screwdriver
Allen wrench
Pipe wrench
Channel-type pliers
Small cold chisel
Ball-peen hammer

Deep-set
ratchet wrench
Masking tape or cloth
Pipe joint compound
Replacement faucet
parts, as needed

A two-handle tub/shower faucet can operate with compression valves, but more often these days they contain cartridges that can be replaced. Unlike a three-handled model, the diverter is a simple gate valve that operated by a lever.

Tips on Replacing a Tub Spout ▸

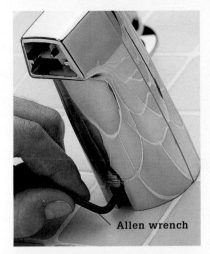

Check underneath tub spout for a small access slot. The slot indicates the spout is held in place with an Allen screw. Remove the screw, using an Allen wrench. Spout will slide off.

Unscrew faucet spout. Use a pipe wrench, or insert a large screwdriver or hammer handle into the spout opening and turn spout counterclockwise.

Spread pipe joint compound on threads of spout nipple before replacing spout.

How to Remove a Deep-set Faucet Valve

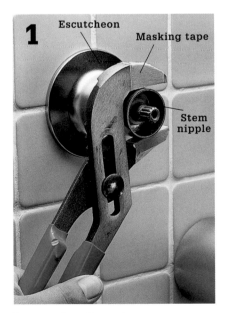

Remove handle and unscrew the escutcheon with channel-type pliers. Pad the jaws of the pliers with masking tape to prevent scratching the escutcheon.

Chip away any mortar surrounding the bonnet nut, using a ball-peen hammer and a small cold chisel.

Unscrew the bonnet nut with a deep-set ratchet wrench. Remove the bonnet nut and stem from the faucet body.

Fixing Single-handle Tub & Shower Faucets

A single-handle tub and shower faucet has one valve that controls both water flow and temperature. Single-handle faucets may be ball-type, cartridge, or disc designs.

If a single-handle control valve leaks or does not function properly, disassemble the faucet, clean the valve, and replace any worn parts. Use the repair techniques described on page 12 for ball-type, or page 13 for ceramic disc. Repairing a single-handle cartridge faucet is shown on the opposite page.

Direction of the water flow to either the tub spout or the showerhead is controlled by a gate diverter. Gate diverters seldom need repair. Occasionally, the lever may break, come loose, or refuse to stay in the up position. If the diverter fails to work properly, replace the tub spout.

Tools & Materials ▶

Screwdriver
Adjustable wrench
Channel-type pliers

Replacement faucet
parts, as needed

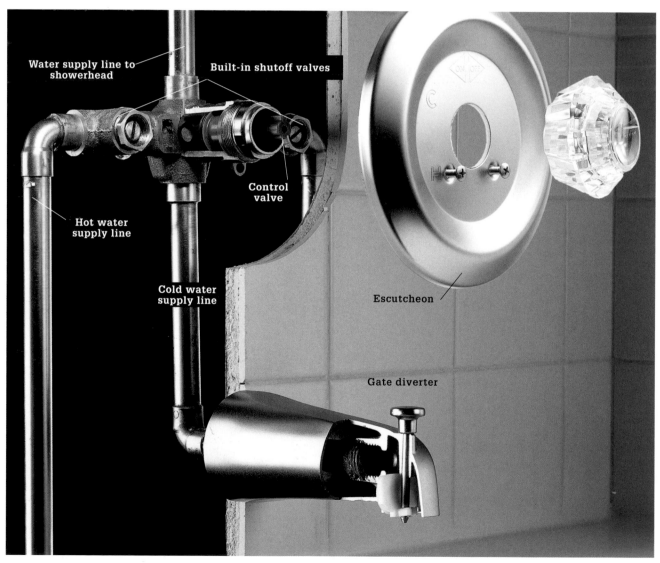

A single-handle tub/shower faucet is the simplest type to operate and to maintain. The handle controls the mixing ratio of both hot and cold water, and the diverter is a simple gate valve.

How to Repair a Single-handle Cartridge Tub & Shower Faucet

Use a screwdriver to remove the handle and escutcheon.

Turn off water supply at the built-in shutoff valves or the main shutoff valve.

Unscrew and remove the retaining ring or bonnet nut, using adjustable wrench.

Remove the cartridge assembly by grasping the end of the valve with channel-type pliers and pulling gently.

Flush the valve body with clean water to remove sediment. Replace any worn O-rings. Reinstall the cartridge and test the valve. If the faucet fails to work properly, replace the cartridge.

5. Installing a New Vanity Faucet

One-piece faucets, with either one or two handles, are the most popular fixtures for bathroom installations.

"Widespread" faucets with separate spout and handles are being installed with increasing frequency, however. Because the handles are connected to the spout with flex tubes that can be 18" or longer, widespread faucets can be arranged in many ways.

Tools & Materials ▸

Hacksaw or tin snips
Channel-type pliers
Pliers
Basin wrench
Adjustable wrench
Screwdriver
Plumber's putty

Teflon tape
Faucet kit
Pipe joint compound
Flexible supply tubes
Heat-proof grease
Loctite basin

Bathroom sink faucets come in two basic styles: the widespread with independent handles and spout (top); and the single-body, deck-mounted version (bottom).

Bathroom Faucet & Drain Hookups

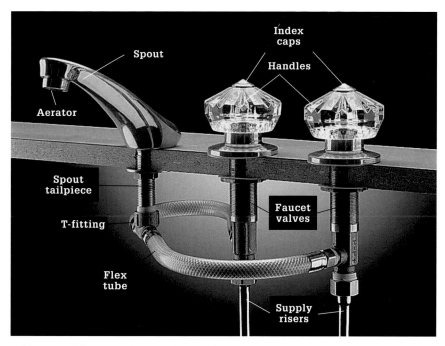

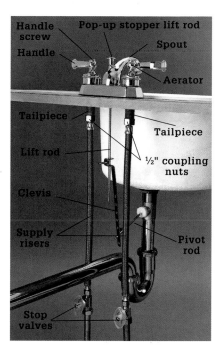

Widespread lavatory faucets have valves that are independent from the spout so they can be configured however you choose, provided that your flex tube connectors are long enough to span the distance.

Single-body lavatory faucets have both valves and the spout permanently affixed to the faucet body. They do not offer flexibility in configurations, but they are very simple to install.

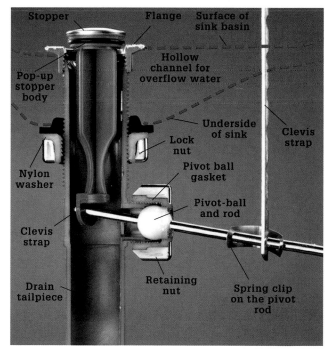

The pop-up stopper fits into the drain opening so the stopper will close tightly against the drain flange when the pop-up handle is lifted up.

The linkage that connects the pop-up stopper to the pop-up handle fits into a male-threaded port in the drain tailpiece. Occasionally the linkage will require adjustment or replacement.

How to Install a Widespread Faucet

Insert the shank of the faucet spout through one of the holes in the sink deck (usually the center hole but you can offset it in one of the end holes if you prefer). If the faucet is not equipped with seals or O-rings for the spout and handles, pack plumber's putty on the undersides before inserting the valves into the deck. *Note: If you are installing the widespread faucet in a new sink deck, drill three holes of the size suggested by the faucet manufacturer.*

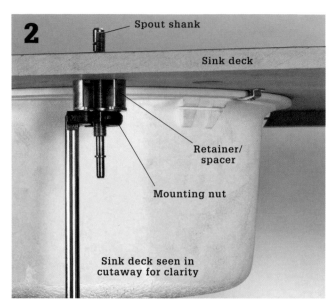

In addition to mounting nuts, many spout valves for widespread faucets have an open-retainer fitting that goes between the underside of the deck and the mounting nut. Others have only a mounting nut. In either case, tighten the mounting nut with pliers or a basin wrench to secure the spout valve. You may need a helper to keep the spout centered and facing forward.

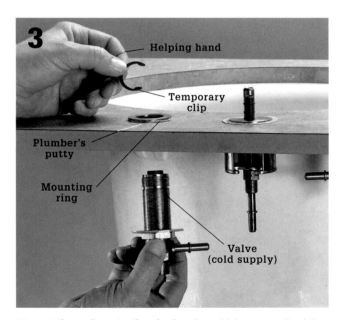

Mount the valves to the deck using whichever method the manufacturer specifies (it varies quite a bit). In the model seen here, a mounting ring is positioned over the deck hole (with plumber's putty seal) and the valve is inserted from below. A clip snaps onto the valve from above to hold it in place temporarily (you'll want a helper for this).

From below, thread the mounting nuts that secure the valves to the sink deck. Make sure the cold water valve (usually has a blue cartridge inside) is in the right-side hole (from the front) and the hot water valve (red cartridge) is in the left hole. Install both valves.

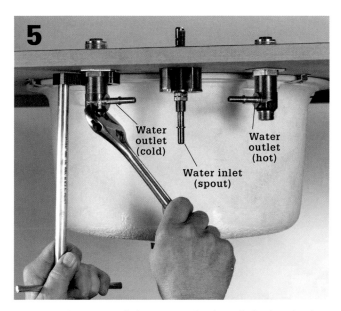

5

Once you've started the nut on the threaded valve shank, secure the valve with a basin wrench, squeezing the lugs where the valve fits against the deck. Use an adjustable wrench to finish tightening the lock nut onto the valve. The valves should be oriented so the water outlets are aimed at the inlet on the spout shank.

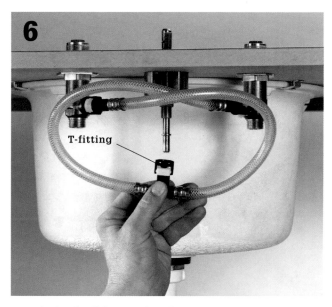

6

Attach the flexible supply tubes (supplied with the faucet) to the water outlets on the valves. Some twist onto the outlets, but others (like the ones above) click into place. The supply hoses meet in a T-fitting that is attached to the water inlet on the spout.

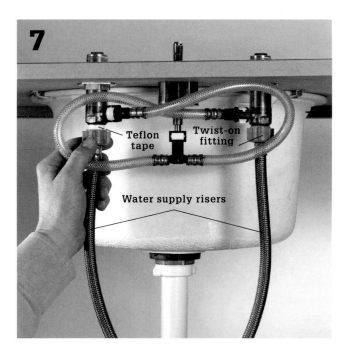

7

Attach flexible braided-metal supply risers to the water stop valves and then attach the tubes to the inlet port on each valve (usually with Teflon tape and a twist-on fitting at the valve end of the supply riser).

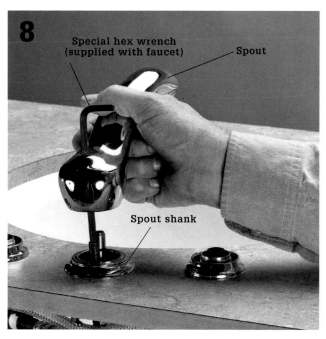

8

Attach the spout. The model shown here comes with a special hex wrench that is threaded through the hole in the spout where the lift rod for the pop-up drain will be located. Once the spout is seated cleanly on the spout shank, you tighten the hex wrench to secure the spout. Different faucets will use other methods to secure the spout to the shank.

(continued)

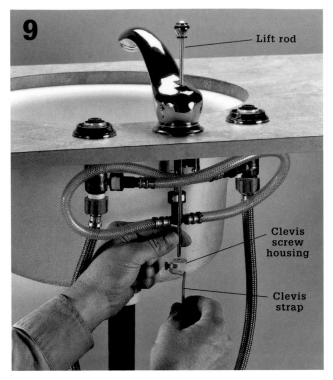

9

Lift rod

Clevis screw housing

Clevis strap

If your sink did not have a pop-up stopper, you'll need to replace the sink drain tailpiece with a pop-up stopper body (often supplied with the faucet). Insert the lift rod through the hole in the back of the spout and, from below, thread the pivot rod through the housing for the clevis screw.

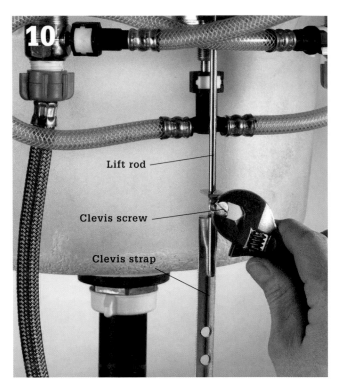

10

Lift rod

Clevis screw

Clevis strap

Attach the clevis strap to the pivot rod that enters the pop-up drain body, and adjust the position of the strap so it raises and lowers properly when the lift rod is pulled up. Tighten the clevis screw at this point. It's hard to fit a screwdriver in here, so you may need to use a wrench or pliers.

11

Attach the faucet handles to the valves using whichever method is required by the faucet manufacturer. Most faucets are designed with registration methods to ensure that the handles are symmetrical and oriented in an ergonomic way once you secure them to the valves.

12

Turn on the water supply and test the faucet. Remove the faucet aerator so any debris in the lines can clear the spout.

Most faucets come with a plastic or foam gasket to seal the bottom of the faucet to the sink deck. These gaskets will not always form a watertight seal. If you want to ensure no splash water gets below the sink, discard the seal and press a ring of plumber's putty into the sealant groove built into the underside of the faucet body.

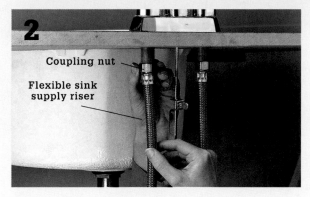

Coupling nut

Flexible sink supply riser

Insert the faucet tailpieces through the holes in the sink. From below, thread washers and mounting nuts over the tailpieces, then tighten the mounting nuts with a basin wrench until snug. Put a dab of pipe joint compound on the threads of the stop valves and thread the metal nuts of the flexible supply risers to these. Wrench tighten about a half-turn past hand tight. Overtightening these nuts will strip the threads. Now tighten the coupling nuts to the faucet tailpieces with a basin wrench.

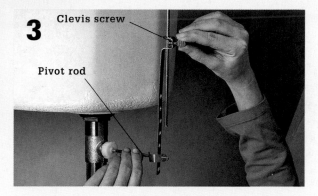

Clevis screw

Pivot rod

Slide the lift rod of the new faucet into its hole behind the spout. Thread it into the clevis past the clevis screw. Push the pivot rod all the way down so the stopper is open. With the lift rod also all the way down, tighten the clevis to the lift rod.

Grease the fluted valve stems with heatproof grease, then put the handles in place. Put a drop of Loctite on each handle screw before tightening it on. (This will keep your handles from coming loose.) Cover each handle screw with the appropriate index cap—Hot or Cold.

Unscrew the aerator from the end of the spout. Turn the hot and cold water taps on full. Turn the water back on at the stop valves and flush out the faucet for a couple of minutes before turning off the water at the faucet. Check the riser connections for drips. Tighten a compression nut only until the drip stops.

How to Install a Pop-up Drain

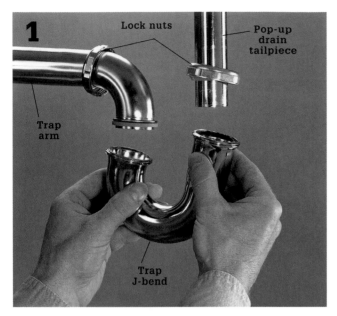

1

Lock nuts

Pop-up drain tailpiece

Trap arm

Trap J-bend

Put a basin under the trap to catch water. Loosen the nuts at the outlet and inlet to the trap J-bend by hand or with channel-type pliers and remove the bend. The trap will slide off the pop-up body tailpiece when the nuts are loose. Keep track of washers and nuts and their up/down orientation by leaving them on the tubes.

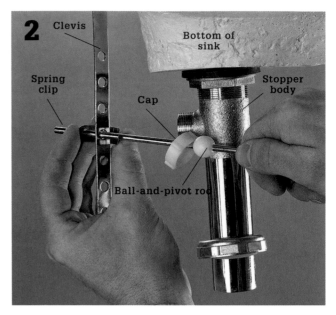

2

Clevis

Bottom of sink

Spring clip

Cap

Stopper body

Ball-and-pivot rod

Unscrew the cap holding the ball-and-pivot rod in the pop-up body and withdraw the ball. Compress the spring clip on the clevis and withdraw the pivot rod from the clevis.

3

Stopper

Flange

Remove the pop-up stopper. Then, from below, remove the lock nut on the stopper body. If needed, keep the flange from turning by inserting a large screwdriver in the drain from the top. Thrust the stopper body up through the hole to free the flange from the basin, and then remove the flange and the stopper body.

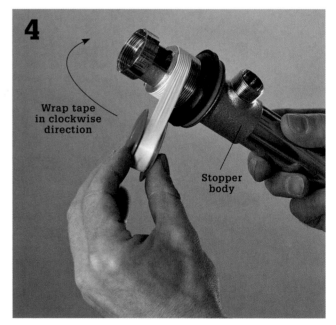

4

Wrap tape in clockwise direction

Stopper body

Clean the drain opening above and below, and then thread the locknut all the way down the new pop-up body, followed by the flat washer and the rubber gasket (beveled side up). Wrap three layers of Teflon tape clockwise onto the top of the threaded body. Make a ½"-dia. snake from plumber's putty, form it into a ring, and stick the ring underneath the drain flange.

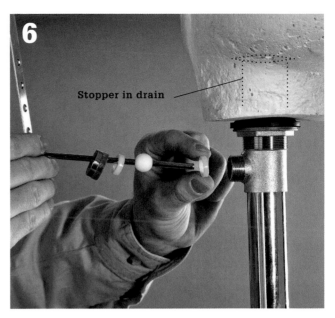

From below, face the pivot rod opening directly back toward the middle of the faucet and pull the body straight down to seat the flange. Thread the locknut/washer assembly up under the sink, then fully tighten the locknut with channel-type pliers. Do not twist the flange in the process, as this can break the putty seal. Clean off the squeezeout of plumber's putty from around the flange.

Drop the pop-up stopper into the drain hole so the hole at the bottom of its post is closest to the back of the sink. Put the beveled nylon washer into the opening in the back of the pop-up body with the bevel facing back.

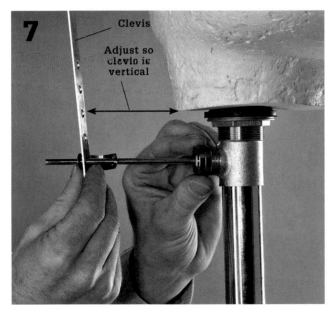

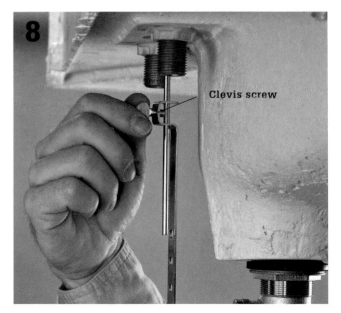

Put the cap behind the ball on the pivot rod as shown. Sandwich a hole in the clevis with the spring clip and thread the long end of the pivot rod through the clip and clevis. Put the ball end of the pivot rod into the pop-up body opening and into the hole in the the stopper stem. Screw the cap on to the pop-up body over the ball.

Loosen the clevis screw holding the clevis to the lift rod. Push the pivot rod all the way down (which fully opens the pop-up stopper). With the lift rod also all the way down, tighten the clevis screw to the rod. If the clevis runs into the top of the trap, cut it short with your hacksaw or tin snips. Reassemble the J-bend trap.

6. Installing a Pedestal Sink

Pedestal sinks move in and out of popularity more frequently than other sink types, but even during times they aren't particularly trendy they retain fairly stable demand. You'll find them most frequently in small half baths, where their little footprint makes them an efficient choice. Designers are also discovering the appeal of tandem pedestal sinks of late, where the smaller profiles allow for his-and-hers sinks that don't dominate visually.

The primary drawback to pedestal sinks is that they don't offer any storage. Their chief practical benefit is that they conceal plumbing some homeowners would prefer not to see.

Pedestal sinks are mounted in two ways. Most of the more inexpensive ones you'll find at home stores are hung in the manner of wall-hung sinks. The pedestal is actually installed after the sink is hung and its purpose is only decorative. But other pedestal sinks (typically on the higher end of the design scale) have structurally important pedestals that do most or all of the bearing for the sink.

Pedestal sinks are available in a variety of styles and are a perfect fit for small half baths. They keep plumbing hidden, lending a neat, contained look to the bathroom.

How to Install a Pedestal Sink

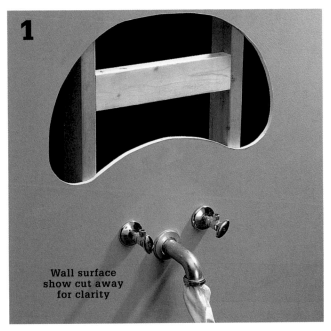

Install 2 × 4 blocking between the wall studs, behind the planned sink location. Cover the wall with water-resistant drywall. Waste and supply lines may need to be moved, depending on the sink.

Set the basin and pedestal in position and brace it with 2 × 4s. Outline the top of the basin on the wall, and mark the base of the pedestal on the floor. Mark reference points on the wall and floor through the mounting holes found on the back of the sink and the bottom of the pedestal.

Set aside the basin and pedestal. Drill pilot holes in the wall and floor at the reference points, then reposition the pedestal. Anchor the pedestal to the floor with lag screws.

Attach the faucet, then set the sink on the pedestal. Align the holes in the back of the sink with the pilot holes drilled in the wall, then drive lag screws and washers into the wall brace using a ratchet wrench. Do not overtighten the screws.

Hook up the drain and supply fittings. Caulk between the back of the sink and the wall when installation is finished.

7. Installing a Wall-Hung Vanity

Think of a wall-mounted sink or vanity cabinet and you're likely to conjure up images of public restrooms where these conveniences are installed to improve access for floor cleaning. However, wall-hung sinks and vanities made for home use are very different from the commercial installations.

Often boasting high design, beautiful modern vanities and sinks come in a variety of styles and materials, including wood, metal, and glass. Some attach with decorative wall brackets that are part of the presentation; others look like standard vanities, just without legs. Install wall-hung sinks and vanities by attaching them securely to studs or wood blocking.

Tools & Materials ▸

Studfinder   Level
Drill   Vanity

Today's wall-hung sinks are stylish and attractive, but they require mounting into studs or added blocking to keep them secure.

How to Install a Wall-Hung Vanity Base

1

Remove the existing sink or fixture and inspect the wall framing. Also determine if plumbing supply and waste lines will need to be moved to accommodate the dimensions of the new fixture. Locate the studs in the sink location with a stud finder.

2

Hold the sink or cabinet in the installation area and check to see if the studs align with the sink or sink bracket mounting holes. If they do, skip to step 3. If the studs do not align, remove the wallboard behind the mounting area. Install 2 × 6 blocking between studs at the locations of the mounting screws. Replace and repair wallboard.

3

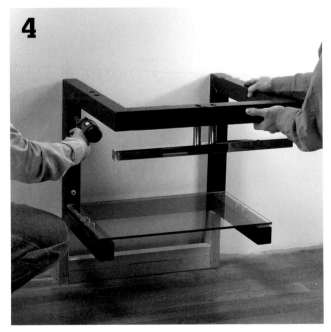

Mark the locations of the mounting holes on the wall using a template or by supporting the sink or vanity against the wall with a temporary brace (made here from scrap 2 × 4s) and marking through the mounting holes.

4

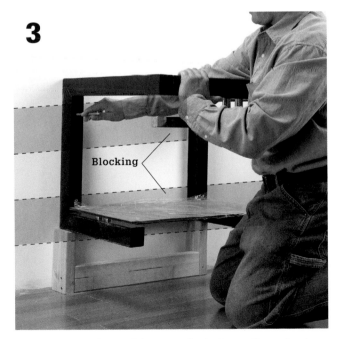

Drill pilot holes at the marks. Have a helper hold the vanity in place while you drive the mounting screws. Hook up the plumbing (see pages 28 to 33).

8. Installing a Vessel Sink

The vessel sink harkens back to the days of washstands and washbowls. Whether it's round, square, or oval, shallow or deep, the vessel sink offers great opportunity for creativity and proudly displays its style. Vessel sinks are a perfect choice for a powder room, where they will have high visibility.

Most vessel sinks can be installed on any flat surface—from a granite countertop to a wall-mounted vanity to an antique dresser. Some sinks are designed to contact the mounting surface only at the drain flange. Others are made to be partially embedded in the surface. Take care to follow the manufacturer's instructions for cutting holes for sinks and faucets.

A beautiful vessel sink demands an equally attractive faucet. Select a tall spout mounted on the countertop or vanity top or a wall-mounted spout to accommodate the height of the vessel. To minimize splashing, spouts should directly flow to the center of the vessel, not down the side. Make sure your faucet is compatible with your vessel choice. Look for a centerset or single-handle model if you'll be custom drilling the countertop—you only need to drill one faucet hole.

Tools & Materials ▸

Jigsaw	Drill
Trowel	Vanity or countertop
Pliers	Vessel sink
Wrench	Pop-up drain
Caulk gun and caulk	P-trap and drain kit
Sponge	Faucet
	Phillips screwdriver

Vessel sinks are available in countless styles and materials, shapes, and sizes. Their one commonality is that they all need to be installed on a flat surface.

Vessel Sink Options

This glass vessel sink embedded in a "floating" glass countertop is a stunning contrast to the strong and attractive wood frame anchoring it to the wall.

The natural stone vessel sink blends elegantly into the stone countertop and is enhanced by the sleek faucet and round mirror.

The stone vessel sink is complemented by the wall-hung faucet. The rich wood vanity on which it's perched adds warmth to the room.

Vitreous china with a glazed enamel finish is an economical and durable choice for a vessel sink (although it is less durable than stone). Because of the flexibility of both the material and the glaze, the design options are virtually unlimited with vitreous china.

How to Install a Vessel Sink

1

Secure the vanity cabinet or other countertop that you'll be using to mount the vessel sink.

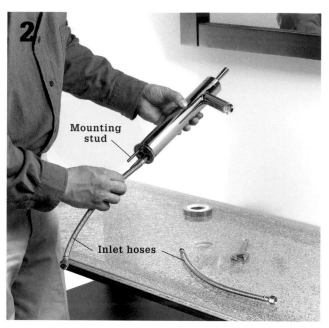

2

Begin hooking up the faucet. Insert the brass mounting stud into the threaded hole in the faucet base with the slotted end facing out. Hand tighten, and then use a screwdriver to tighten another half turn. Insert the inlet hoses into the faucet body and hand tighten. Use an adjustable wrench to tighten another half turn. Do not overtighten.

Mounting stud

Inlet hoses

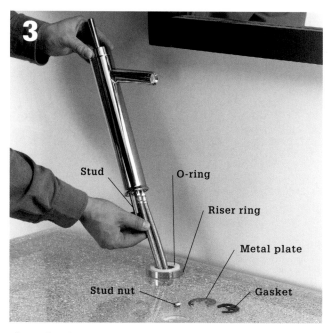

3

Stud

O-ring

Riser ring

Metal plate

Stud nut

Gasket

Place the riser ring on top of the O-ring over the faucet cutout in the countertop. From underneath, slide the rubber gasket and the metal plate over the mounting stud. Thread the mounting stud nut onto the mounting stud and hand tighten. Use an adjustable wrench to tighten another half turn.

4

To install the sink and pop-up drain, first place the small metal ring between two O-rings and place over the drain cutout.

5

Place the vessel bowl on top of the O-rings. In this installation, the vessel is not bonded to the countertop.

6

Put the small rubber gasket over the drain hole in the vessel. From the top, push the pop-up assembly through the drain hole.

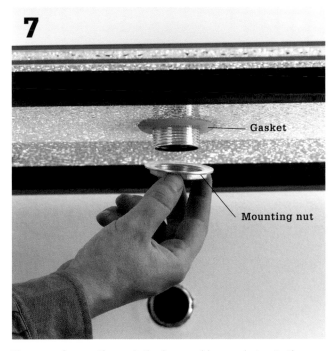

7

Gasket

Mounting nut

From underneath, push the large rubber gasket onto the threaded portion of the pop-up assembly. Thread the nut onto the pop-up assembly and tighten. Use an adjustable wrench or basin wrench to tighten an additional half turn. Thread the tailpiece onto the pop-up assembly.

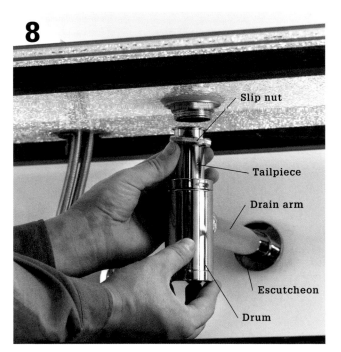

8

Slip nut

Tailpiece

Drain arm

Escutcheon

Drum

Install the drum trap. Loosen the rings on the top and outlet of the drum trap. Slide the drum trap top hole over the tailpiece. Slide the drain arm into the side outlet, with the flat side of the rubber gasket facing away from the trap. Insert the drain arm into the wall outlet. Hand tighten the rings.

9. Installing an Integral Vanity Top

Most bathroom countertops installed today are integral (one-piece) sink-countertop units made from cultured marble or other solid materials, like solid surfacing. Integral sink-countertops are convenient, and many are inexpensive, but style and color options are limited.

Some remodelers and designers still prefer the distinctive look of a custom-built countertop with a self-rimming sink basin, which gives you a much greater selection of styles and colors. Installing a self-rimming sink is very simple.

Tools & Materials ▸

Pencil
Scissors
Carpenter's level
Screwdriver
Channel-type pliers
Ratchet wrench
Basin wrench

Cardboard
Masking tape
Plumber's putty
Lag screws
Tub and tile caulk
Pipe dope

Integral sink-countertops are made in standard sizes to fit common vanity widths. Because the sink and countertop are cast from the same material, integral sink-countertops do not leak, and do not require extensive caulking and sealing.

How to Install a Vanity Cabinet

Set the sink-countertop unit onto sawhorses. Attach the faucet and slip the drain lever through the faucet body. Place a ring of plumber's putty around the drain flange, then insert the flange in the drain opening.

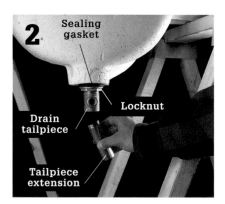

Thread the locknut and sealing gasket onto the drain tailpiece, then insert the tailpiece into the drain opening and screw it onto the drain flange. Tighten the locknut securely. Attach the tailpiece extension. Insert the pop-up stopper linkage.

Place a small amount of pipe dope on all threads. Apply a layer of tub and tile caulk (or adhesive, if specified by the countertop manufacturer) to the top edges of the cabinet vanity, and to any corner braces.

Center the sink-countertop unit over the vanity so the overhang is equal on both sides and the backsplash of the countertop is flush with the wall. Press the countertop evenly into the caulk.

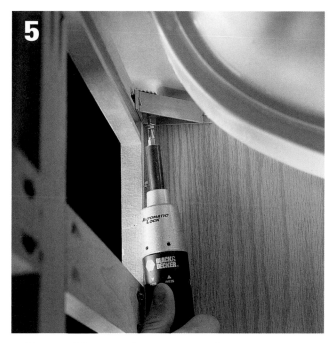

Cabinets with corner braces: Secure the countertop to the cabinet by driving a mounting screw through each corner brace and up into the countertop. *Note: Cultured marble and other hard countertops require predrilling and a plastic screw sleeve.*

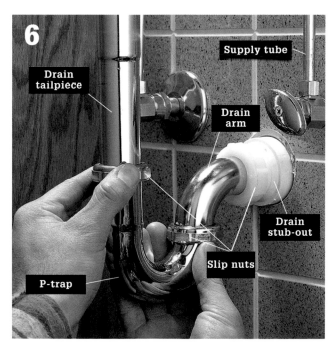

Attach the drain arm to the drain stub-out in the wall, using a slip nut. Attach one end of the P-trap to the drain arm, and the other to the tailpiece of the sink drain, using slip nuts. Connect supply tubes to the faucet tailpieces.

Seal the gap between the backsplash and the wall with tub and tile caulk.

10. Replacing a Toilet

You can replace a poorly functioning or inefficient toilet with a high-efficiency, high-quality new toilet in just a single afternoon. All toilets made since 1996 have been required to use 1.6 gallons or less per flush, which has been a huge challenge for the industry. Today, the most evolved 1.6-gallon toilets have wide passages behind the bowl and wide (3") flush valve openings—features that facilitate short, powerful flushes. This means fewer second flushes and fewer clogged toilets. These problems were common complaints of the first generation of 1.6-gallon toilets and continue to beleaguer inferior models today. See what toilets are available at your local home center in your price range, then go online and see what other consumers' experiences with those models have been. New toilets often go through a "de-bugging" stage when problems with leaks and malfunctioning parts are more common. Your criteria should include ease of installation, good flush performance, and reliability. With a little research, you should be able to purchase and install a high-functioning economical gravity-flush toilet that will serve you well for years to come.

Tools & Materials ▸

Adjustable wrench	Supply tube
Bucket and sponge	Teflon tape
Channel-type pliers	Toilet seat bolts
Hacksaw	Toilet seat
Penetrating oil	Towels
Pliers	Utility knife
Putty knife	Wax ring
Rubber gloves	without flange
Screwdriver	Wax ring with flange

Replacing a toilet is simple, and the latest generation of 1.6-gallon water-saving toilets has overcome the performance problems of earlier models.

Choosing a New Toilet

Toilets have changed in recent years. There's a toilet to fit every style. You can even buy a square or stainless steel toilet, among many other new options. The new designs are efficient, durable, and less susceptible to clogs.

A toilet's style is partly affected by the way it's built. You have a number of options from which to choose:

Two-piece toilets have a separate water tank and bowl.

One-piece toilets have a tank and bowl made of one seamless unit.

Elongated bowls are roughly 2" longer than regular bowls.

Elevated toilets have higher seats, generally 18", rather than the standard 15".

You have a choice of two basic types of flush mechanisms: gravity- and pressure-assisted.

Gravity-assisted toilets allow water to rush down from an elevated tank into the toilet bowl. Federal law mandates that new toilets consume no more than 1.6 gallons of water per flush, less than half the volume used by older styles.

Pressure-assisted toilets rely on either compressed air or water pumps to boost flushing power.

Dual-flush systems feature two flush buttons on the top of the tank, allowing you to select either an 8-ounce flush for liquids or a 1.6-gallon flush for solids.

Toilets are available in a variety of styles and colors to suit almost any decor. Two-piece toilets are generally cheaper and come in a great assortment of styles and colors. Many high end models have a matching bidet available.

Gravity-assisted toilets are now designed with taller tanks and steeper bowl walls to increase the effects of gravity.

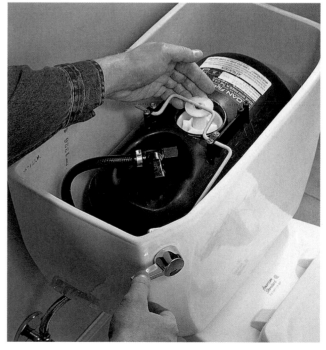

Pressure-assisted toilets are more expensive than standard toilets, but they can reduce your water usage significantly. The flush mechanism of a pressure-assisted toilet boosts the flushing power by using either compressed air or water pumps.

How to Remove a Toilet

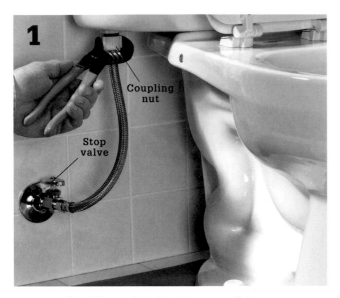

Remove the old supply tube. First, turn off the water at the stop valve. Flush the toilet, holding the handle down for a long flush, and sponge out the tank. Unthread the coupling nut for the water supply below the tank using channel-type pliers. Use a wet/dry vac to clear any remaining water out of the tank and bowl.

Grip each tank bolt nut with a box wrench or pliers and loosen it as you stabilize each tank bolt from inside the tank with a large slotted screwdriver. If the nuts are stuck, apply penetrating oil to the nut and let it sit before trying to remove them again. You may also cut the tank bolts between the tank and the bowl with an open-ended hacksaw. Remove and discard the tank.

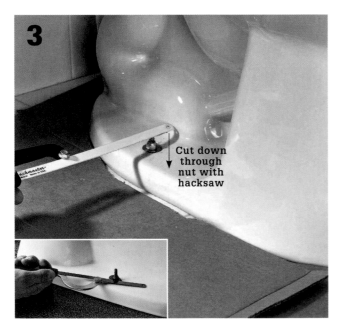

Remove the nuts that hold the bowl to the floor. First, pry off the bolt covers with a screwdriver. Use a socket wrench, locking pliers, or your channel-type pliers to loosen the nuts on the tank bolts. Apply penetrating oil and let it sit if the nuts are stuck, then take them off. As a last resort, cut the bolts off with a hacksaw by first cutting down through one side of the nut. Tilt the toilet bowl over and remove it.

Tip ▸

Removing an old wax ring is one of the more disgusting jobs you'll encounter in the plumbing universe (the one you see here is actually in relatively good condition). Work a stiff putty knife underneath the plastic flange of the ring (if you can) and start scraping. In many cases the wax ring will come off in chunks. Discard each chunk right away—they stick to everything. If you're left with a lot of residue, scrub with mineral spirits. Once clean, stuff a rag in a bag in the drain opening to block sewer gas.

How to Install a Toilet

1

Clean and inspect the old closet flange. Look for breaks or wear. Also inspect the flooring around the flange. If either the flange or floor is worn or damaged, repair the damage. Use a rag and mineral spirits to completely remove residue from the old wax ring. Place a rag-in-a-bag into the opening to block odors.

Tip ▶

If you will be replacing your toilet flange or if your existing flange can be unscrewed and moved, orient the new flange so the slots are parallel to the wall. This allows you to insert bolts under the slotted areas, which are much stronger than the areas at the ends of the curved grooves.

2

Insert new tank bolts (don't reuse old ones) into the openings in the closet flange. Make sure the heads of the bolts are oriented to catch the maximum amount of flange material.

3

Remove the wax ring and apply it to the underside of the bowl, around the horn. Remove the protective covering. Do not touch the wax ring. It is very sticky. Remove the rag-in-a-bag.

(continued)

Lower the bowl onto the flange, taking care not to disturb the wax ring. The holes in the bowl base should align perfectly with the tank bolts. Add a washer and tighten a nut on each bolt. Hand tighten each nut and then use channel-type pliers to further tighten the nuts. Alternate back and forth between nuts until the bowl is secure. *Do not overtighten.*

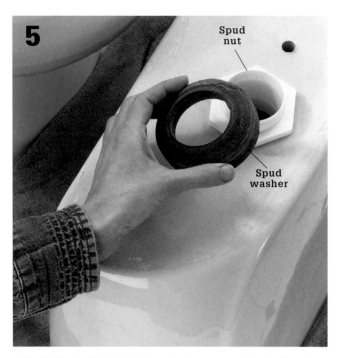

Attach the toilet tank. Some tanks come with a flush valve and a fill valve preinstalled. For models that do not have this, insert the flush valve through the tank opening and tighten a spud nut over the threaded end of the valve. Place a foam spud washer on top of the spud nut.

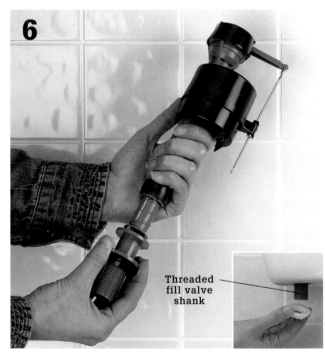

Adjust the fill valve as directed by the manufacturer to set the correct tank water level height and install the valve inside the tank. Hand tighten the nylon lock nut that secures the valve to the tank (inset photo) and then tighten it further with channel-type pliers.

With the tank lying on its back, thread a rubber washer onto each tank bolt and insert it into the bolt holes from inside the tank. Then, thread a brass washer and hex nut onto the tank bolts from below and tighten them to a quarter turn past hand tight. Do not overtighten.

8

Position the tank on the bowl, spud washer on opening, bolts through bolt holes. Put a rubber washer, followed by a brass washer and a wing nut, on each bolt and tighten these up evenly.

Intermediate
nut

9

You may stabilize the bolts with a large slotted screwdriver from inside the tank, but tighten the nuts, not the bolts. You may press down a little on a side, the front, or the rear of the tank to level it as you tighten the nuts by hand. Do not overtighten and crack the tank. The tank should be level and stable when you're done. Do not overtighten.

10

Hook up the water supply by connecting the supply tube to the threaded fill valve with the coupling nut provided. Turn on the water and test for leaks. Do not overtighten.

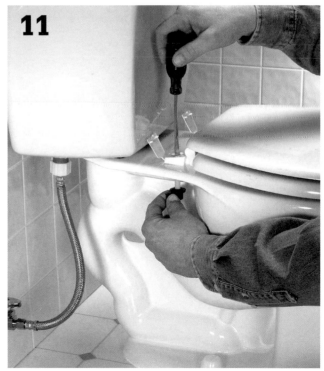

11

Attach the toilet seat by threading the plastic or brass bolts provided with the seat through the openings on the back of the rim and attaching nuts.

11. Installing Sliding Tub Doors

Curtains on your bathtub shower are a hassle. If you forget to tuck them inside the tub, water flows freely onto your bathroom floor. If you forget to slide them closed, mildew sets up shop in the folds. And every time you brush against them they stick to your skin. Shower curtains certainly don't add much elegance or charm to a dream bath. Neither does a deteriorated door. Clean up the look of your bathroom, and even give it an extra touch of elegance, with a new sliding tub door.

When shopping for a sliding tub door, you have a choice of framed or frameless. A framed door is edged in metal. The metal framing is typically aluminum but is available in many finishes, including those that resemble gold, brass, or chrome. Glass options are also plentiful. You can choose between frosted or pebbled glass, clear, mirrored, tinted, or patterned glass. Doors can be installed on ceramic tile walls or through a fiberglass tub surround.

Tools & Materials ▸

Measuring tape	Masonry bit
Pencil	for tile wall
Hacksaw	Phillips screwdriver
Miter box	Caulk gun
Level	Masking tape
Drill	Silicone sealant
Center punch	& remover
Razor blade	Tub door kit
Marker	Masking tape

A sliding tub door framed in aluminum gives the room a sleek, clean look and is just one of the available options.

How to Install Sliding Tub Doors

1

Remove the existing door and inspect the walls. Use a razor blade to cut sealant from tile and metal surfaces. Do not use a razor blade on fiberglass surfaces. Remove remaining sealant by scraping or pulling. Use a silicone sealant remover to remove all residue. Remove shower curtain rods, if present. Check the walls and tub ledge for plumb and level.

2

Measure the distance between the finished walls along the top of the tub ledge. Refer to the manufacturer's instructions for figuring the track dimensions. For the product seen here, $3/16$" is subtracted from the measurement to calculate the track dimensions.

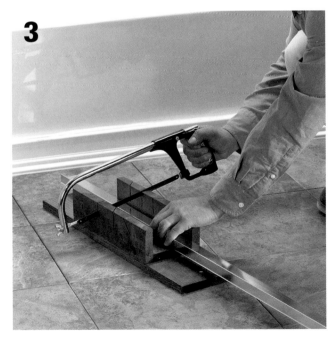

3

Using a hacksaw and a miter box, carefully cut the track to the proper dimension. Center the track on the bathtub ledge with the taller side out and so the gaps are even at each end. Tape into position with masking tape.

4

Place a wall channel against the wall with the longer side out and slide into place over the track so they overlap. Use a level to check the channel for plumb, and then mark the locations of the mounting holes on the wall with a marker. Repeat for the other wall channel. Remove the track.

(continued)

5

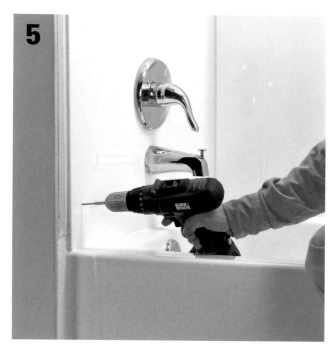

Drill mounting holes for the wall channel at the marked locations. In ceramic tile, nick the surface of the tile with a center punch, use a ¼" masonry bit to drill the hole, and then insert the included wall anchors. For fiberglass surrounds, use a ⅛" drill bit; wall anchors are not necessary.

6

Apply a bead of silicone sealant along the joint between the tub and the wall at the ends of the track. Apply a minimum ¼" bead of sealant along the outside leg of the track underside.

7

Position the track on the tub ledge and against the wall. Attach the wall channels using the provided screws. Do not use caulk on the wall channels at this time.

8

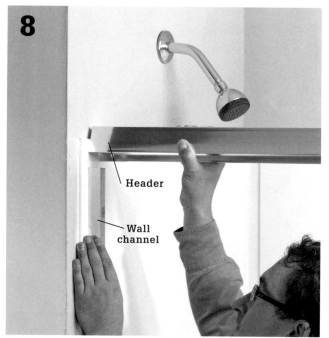

Header

Wall channel

Cut and install the header. At a location above the tops of the wall channels, measure the distance between the walls. Refer to the manufacturer's instructions for calculating the header length. For the door seen here, the length is the distance between the walls minus 1⁄16". Measure the header and carefully cut it to length using a hacksaw and a miter box. Slide the header down on top of the wall channels until seated.

9

Mount the rollers in the roller mounting holes. To begin, use the second-from-the-top roller mounting holes. Follow the manufacturer's instructions for spacer or washer placement and orientation.

10

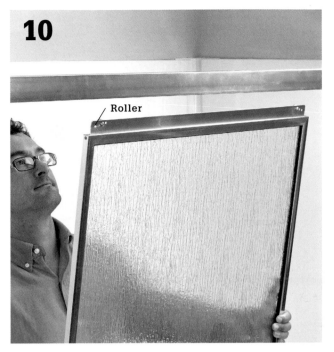

Roller

Carefully lift the inner panel by the sides and place the rollers on the inner roller track. Roll the door toward the shower end of the tub. The edge of the panel should touch both rubber bumpers. If it doesn't, remove the door and move the rollers to different holes. Drive the screws by hand to prevent overtightening.

11

Lift the outer panel by the sides with the towel bar facing out from the tub. Place the outer rollers over the outer roller track. Slide the door to the end opposite the shower end of the tub. If the door does not contact both bumpers, remove the door and move the rollers to different mounting holes.

12

Apply a bead of clear silicone sealant to the inside seam of the wall and wall channel at both ends and to the U-shaped joint of the track and wall channels. Smooth the sealant with a fingertip dipped in water.

12. Installing a 3-Piece Tub Surround

No one wants bathroom fixtures that are aging or yellowed from years of use. A shiny new tub surround can add sparkle and freshness to your dream bath.

Tub surrounds come in many different styles, materials, and price ranges. Choose the features you want and measure your existing bathtub surround for sizing. Surrounds typically come in three or five pieces. A three-panel surround is being installed here, but the process is similar for five-panel systems.

Surface preparation is important for good glue adhesion. Plastic tiles and wallpaper must be removed and textured plaster must be sanded smooth. Surrounds can be installed over ceramic tile that is well attached and in good condition, but it must be sanded and primed. All surfaces must be primed with a water-based primer.

Tools & Materials ▸

Jigsaw	Adhesive
Hole saw	Screwdriver
Drill	Adjustable wrench
Measuring tape	Pry bar
Level	Hammer
Caulking gun	3-piece tub surround
Primer	

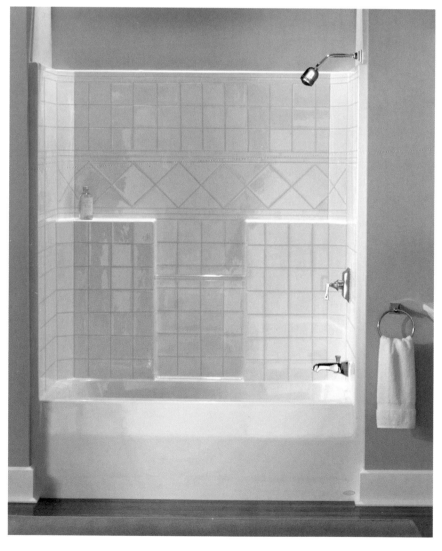

Three-piece tub surrounds are inexpensive and come in many colors and styles. The typical unit has two end panels and a back panel that overlap in the corners to form a watertight seal. They are formed from fiberglass, PVC, acrylic, or proprietary resin-based polymers. Five piece versions are also available and typically have more features such as integral soap shelves and even cabinets.

How to Install a 3-Piece Tub Surround

Remove the old plumbing fixtures and wallcoverings in the tub area. In some cases you can attach surround panels to old tileboard or even tile, but it is generally best to remove the wallcoverings down to the studs if you can, so you may inspect for leaks or damage.

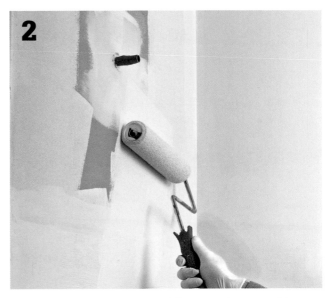

Replace the wallcoverings with appropriate materials, such as water and mold-resistant wallboard or cementboard (for ceramic tile installations). Make sure the new wall surfaces are smooth and flat. Some surround kit manufacturers recommend that you apply a coat of primer to sheet goods such as greenboard to create a better bonding surface for the panel adhesive.

Test-fit the panels before you start; the tub may have settled unevenly or the walls may be out of plumb. Check the manufacturer's directions for distinguishing right and left panels. Place a panel in position on the tub ledge. Use a level across the top of the panel to determine if it is level. Create a vertical reference line to mark the edge of the panel on the plumbing end.

Test-fitting Tip ▶

Ensure a perfect fit by taping the surround panels to the walls in the tub area. Make sure the tops are level when the overlap seams are aligned and that you have a consistent ⅛" gap between the panel bottoms and the tub flange. Mark the panels for cutting if necessary and, once the panels have been removed, make any adjustments to the walls that are needed.

(continued)

4

Some kits are created to fit a range of bathtub dimensions. After performing the test fit, check the fitting instructions to see if you need to trim any of the pieces. Follow the manufacturer's instructions for cutting. Here, we had to cut the corner panels because the instructions advise not to overlap the back or side panel over the corner panels by more than 3". Cut panels using a jigsaw and a fine-tooth blade that is appropriate for cutting fiberglass or acrylic tileboard. The cut panels should be overlapped by panels with factory edges.

5

Measure and mark the location of the faucets, spout, and shower outlets. Measure in from the vertical reference line (made in step 3) and up from the top of the tub ledge. Re-measure for accuracy, as any cuts to the surround are final. Place the panel face-up on a sheet of plywood. Mark the location of the holes. Cut the holes ½" larger than the pipe diameter. If your faucet has a recessed trim plate (escutcheon), cut the hole to fit the recess. Using a hole saw or a jigsaw, cut out the plumbing outlets.

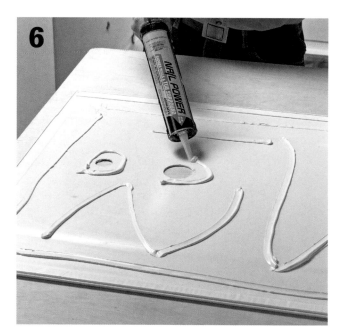

6

Install the plumbing end panel, test-fitting first. In this surround, the end panels are installed first. Apply adhesive to the back of the plumbing panel. Circle the plumbing outlet holes 1" from the edge. Follow the manufacturer's application pattern. Do not apply adhesive closer than 1" to the double-sided tape or the bottom edge of the panel.

7

Remove the protective backing from the tape. Carefully lift the panel by the edges and place against the corner and top of the tub ledge. Press firmly from top to bottom in the corner, then throughout the panel.

8

Test-fit the opposite end panel and make any necessary adjustments. Apply the adhesive, remove the protective backing from the tape, and put in place. Apply pressure to the corner first from top to bottom, and then apply pressure throughout.

9

Apply adhesive to the back panel following the manufacturer's instructions. Maintain a 1" space between adhesive tape and the bottom of the panel. Remove protective backing from the tape. Lift the panel by the edges and carefully center between the two end panels. When positioned, firmly press in place from top to bottom.

10

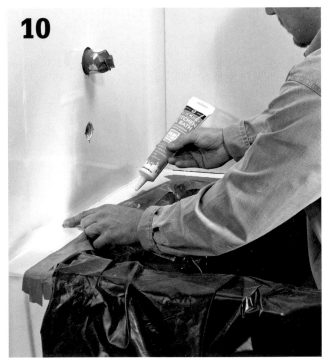

Apply caulk to the bottom and top edges of the panels and at panel joints. Dip your fingertip in water and use it to smooth the caulk to a uniform bead.

11

Apply silicone caulk to escutcheons or trim plates and reinstall them. Allow a minimum of 24 hours for caulk and adhesive to dry thoroughly before using the shower or tub.

13. Unclogging a Toilet

The toilet is clogged and has overflowed. Have patience. Now is the time for considered action. A second flush is a tempting but unnecessary gamble. First, do damage control. Mop up the water if there's been a spill. Next, consider the nature of the clog. Is it entirely "natural" or might a foreign object be contributing to the congestion? Push a natural blockage down the drain with a plunger. A foreign object should be removed, if possible, with a closet auger. Pushing anything more durable than toilet paper into the sewer may create a more serious blockage in your drain and waste system.

If the tub, sink, and toilet all back up at once, the branch drainline that serves all the bathroom fixtures is probably blocked and your best recourse is to call a drain clearing service.

Tools & Materials ▸

Towels
Closet auger

Plunger with foldout
skirt (force cup)

A blockage in the toilet bowl leaves flush water from the tank nowhere to go but on the floor.

Drain Clearers ▸

The home repair marketplace is filled with gadgets and gimmicks, as well as well-established products, that are intended to clear drains of all types. Some are caustic chemicals, some are natural enzymes, others are more mechanical in nature. Some help, some are worthless, some can even make the problem worse. Nevertheless, if you are the type of homeowner who is enamored with new products and the latest solutions, you may enjoy testing out new drain cleaners as they become available. In this photo, for example, you'll see a relatively new product that injects blasts of compressed CO_2 directly into your toilet, sink, or tub drain to dislodge clogs. It does not cause any chemicals to enter the waste stream, and the manufacturers claim the CO_2 blast is very gentle and won't damage pipes. As with any new product, use it with caution. But if a plunger or a snake isn't working, it could save you the cost of a house call.

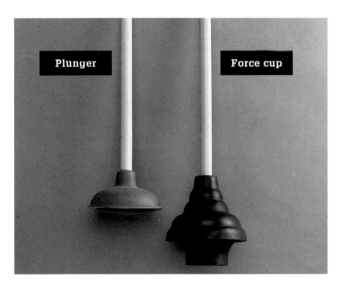

The trap is the most common catching spot for toilet clogs, Once the clog forms, flushing the toilet cannot generate enough water power to clear the trap, so flush water backs up. Traps on modern 1.6-gallon toilets have been redesigned to larger diameters and are less prone to clogs than the first generation of 1.6-gallon toilets.

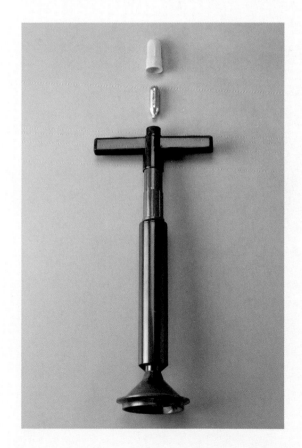

Not all plungers were created equal. The standard plunger (left) is simply an inverted rubber cup and is used to plunge sinks, tubs, and showers. The flanged plunger, also called a force cup, is designed to get down into the trap of a toilet drain. You can fold the flange up into the flanged plunger cup and use it as a standard plunger.

Plunger

Force cup

How to Plunge a Clogged Toilet

Plunging is the easiest way to remove "natural" blockages. Take time to lay towels around the base of the toilet and remove other objects to a safe, dry location, since plunging may result in splashing. Often, allowing a very full toilet to sit for twenty or thirty minutes will permit some of the water to drain to a less precarious level.

Tip ▶

A flanged plunger (force cup) fits into the mouth of the toilet trap and creates a tight seal so you can build up enough pressure in front of the plunger to dislodge the blockage and send it on its way.

There should be enough water in the bowl to completely cover the plunger. Fold out the skirt from inside the plunger to form a better seal with the opening at the base of the bowl. Pump the plunger vigorously half-a-dozen times, take a rest, and then repeat. Try this for 10 to 15 cycles.

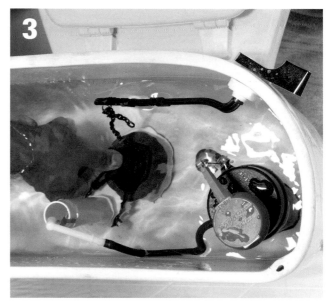

If you force enough water out of the bowl that you are unable to create suction with the plunger, put a controlled amount of water in the bowl by lifting up on the flush valve in the tank. Resume plunging. When you think the drain is clear, you can try a controlled flush, with your hand ready to close the flush valve should the water threaten to spill out of the bowl. Once the blockage has cleared, dump a five-gallon pail of water into the toilet to blast away any residual debris.

How to Clear Clogs with a Closet Auger

Place the business end of the auger firmly in the bottom of the toilet bowl with the auger tip fully withdrawn. A rubber sleeve will protect the porcelain at the bottom bend of the auger. The tip will be facing back and up, which is the direction the toilet trap takes.

Tip ▸

A closet auger is a semirigid cable housed in a tube. The tube has a bend at the end so it can be snaked through a toilet trap (without scratching it) to snag blockages.

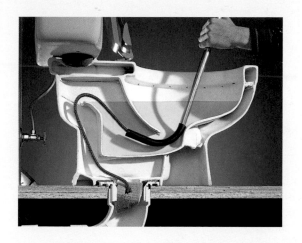

Rotate the handle on the auger housing clockwise as you push down on the rod, advancing the rotating auger tip up into the back part of the trap. You may work the cable backward and forward as needed, but keep the rubber boot of the auger firmly in place in the bowl. When you feel resistance, indicating you've snagged the object, continue rotating the auger counterclockwise as you withdraw the cable and the object.

Fully retract the auger until you have recovered the object. This can be frustrating at times, but it is still a much easier task than the alternative—to remove the toilet and go fishing.

14. Replacing a Toilet Flange

If your toilet rocks it will eventually leak. The rocking means that the bolts are no longer holding the toilet securely to the floor. If you have tightened the bolts and it still rocks, it is possible that a bolt has broken a piece of the flange off and is no longer able to hold. Rocking might also be because an ongoing leak has weakened the floor and it is now uneven. Whatever the reason, a rocking toilet needs to be fixed.

If your flange is connected to cast iron piping, use a repair flange. This has a rubber compression ring that will seal the new flange to the cast iron pipe.

Tools & Materials ▸

Drill	#10 stainless steel
Wrench	flathead wood
Internal pipe cutter	screws
Solvent-glue	Marker

Use a flange repair kit for a quick fix to a broken flange. The new flange piece from the kit is simply screwed to the floor after it has been oriented correctly over the broken flange.

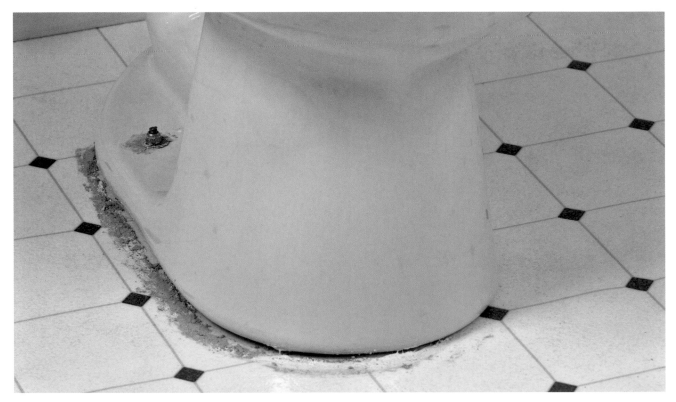

Toilets that rock often only need to have the nuts on the closet bolts tightened. But if you need to tighten the bolts on an ongoing basis, you very likely have a problem with the closet flange.

How to Replace a PVC Closet Flange

Begin by removing the toilet and wax ring. Cut the pipe just below the bottom of the flange using an internal pipe cutter (inset, available at plumbing supply stores). Remove the flange.

New pipe

Repair Coupling

If your flange is attached to a closet bend you will need to open up the floor around the toilet to get at the horizontal pipe connecting the bend to the stack to make the repair. If it is connected to a length of vertical plastic pipe, use a repair coupling and a short length of pipe to bring the pipe back up to floor level. Glue the new pipe into the repair coupling first and allow it to set. Clean the old pipe thoroughly before gluing.

Cut the replacement pipe flush with the floor. Dry-fit the new flange into the pipe. Turn the flange until the side cut-out screw slots are parallel to the wall. (Do not use the curved keyhole slots, as they are not as strong.) Draw lines to mark the location of the slots on the floor.

Prime and solvent-glue the pipe and flange, inserting the flange slightly off the marks and twisting it to proper alignment. Secure the flange to the floor with #10 stainless steel flathead wood screws.

15. Unclogging Tub & Shower Drains

Tub or shower not draining? First, make sure it's only the tub or shower. If your sink is plugged, too, it may be a coincidence or it may be that a common branch line is plugged. A sure sign of this is when water drains from the sink into the tub. This could require the help of a drain cleaning service, or a drum trap that services both the sink and tub needs cleaning.

If the toilet also can't flush (or worse, water comes into the tub when you flush the toilet), then the common drain to all your bathroom fixtures is plugged. Call a drain cleaning service. If you suspect the problem is only with your tub or shower, then read on. We'll show you how to clear drainlines and clean and adjust two types of tub stopper mechanisms. Adjusting the mechanism can also help with the opposite problem: a tub that drains when you're trying to take a bath.

As with bathroom sinks, tub and shower drain pipes may become clogged with soap and hair. The drain stopping mechanisms can also require cleaning and adjustment.

Tools & Materials ▸

Phillips Screwdriver	Toothbrush
Plunger	Needlenose pliers
Scrub brush	Dishwashing brush
White Vinager	Heatproof grease

Maintenance Tip ▸

Like bathroom sinks, tubs and showers face an ongoing onslaught from soap and hair. When paired, this pesky combination is a sure-fire source of clogs. The soap scum coagulates as it is washed down the drain and binds the hair together in a mass that grows larger with every shower or bath. To nip these clogs in the bud, simply pour boiling hot clean water down the drain from time to time to melt the soapy mass and wash the binder away.

Using Hand Augers ▸

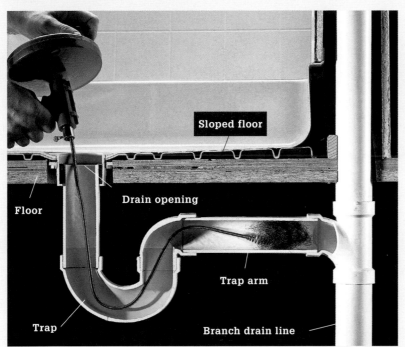

Floor

Sloped floor

Drain opening

Trap arm

Trap

Branch drain line

On shower drains, feed the head of the auger in through the drain opening after removing the strainer. Crank the handle of the auger to extend the cable and the auger head down into the trap and, if the clog is farther downline, toward the branch drain. When clearing any drain, it is always better to retrieve the clog than to push it farther downline.

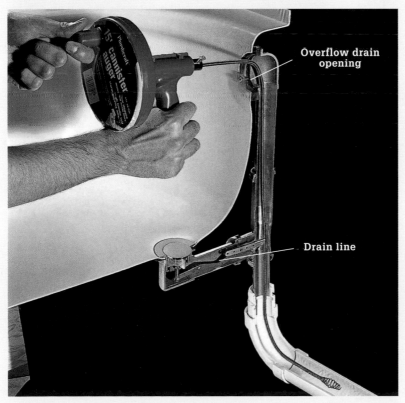

Overflow drain opening

Drain line

On combination tub/showers, it's generally easiest to insert the auger through the overflow opening after removing the coverplate and lifting out the drain linkage. Crank the handle of the auger to extend the cable and the auger head down into the trap and, if the clog is farther downline, toward the branch drain. When clearing any drain, it is always better to retrieve the clog than to push it farther downline.

How to Fix a Plunger-Type Drain

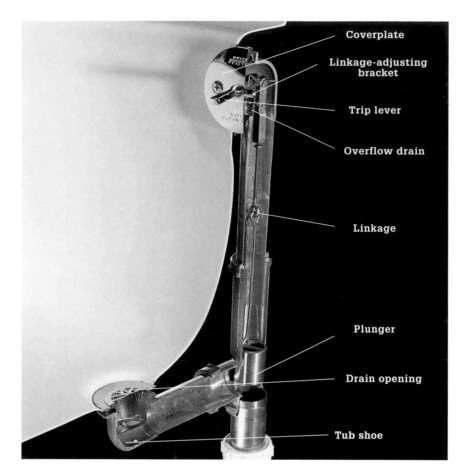

Coverplate

Linkage-adjusting bracket

Trip lever

Overflow drain

Linkage

Plunger

Drain opening

Tub shoe

A plunger-type tub drain has a simple grate over the drain opening and a behind-the-scenes plunger stopper. Remove the screws on the overflow coverplate with a slotted or Phillips screwdriver. Pull the coverplate, linkage, and plunger from the overflow opening.

Clean hair and soap off the plunger with a scrub brush. Mineral buildup is best tackled with white vinegar and a toothbrush or a small wire brush.

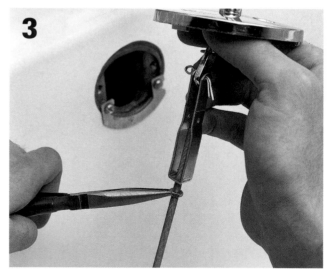

Adjust the plunger. If your tub isn't holding water with the plunger down, it's possible the plunger is hanging too high to fully block water from the tub shoe. Loosen the locknut with needlenose pliers, then screw the rod down about ⅛". Tighten the locknut down. If your tub drains poorly, the plunger may be set too low. Loosen the locknut and screw the rod in an ⅛" before retightening the locknut.

How to Fix a Pop-up Drain

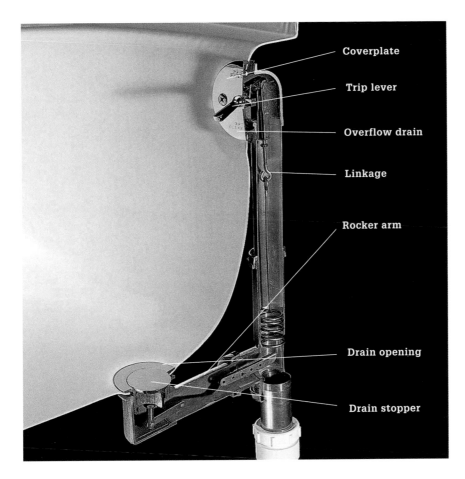

- Coverplate
- Trip lever
- Overflow drain
- Linkage
- Rocker arm
- Drain opening
- Drain stopper

1

Raise the trip lever to the open position. Pull the stopper and rocker arm assembly from the drain. Clean off soap and hair with a dishwashing brush in a basin of hot water. Clean off mineral deposits with a toothbrush or small wire brush and white vinegar.

2

Remove the screws from the cover plate. Pull the trip lever and the linkage from the overflow opening. Clean off soap and hair with a brush in a basin of hot water. Remove mineral buildup with white vinegar and a wire brush. Lubricate moving parts of the linkage and rocker arm mechanism with heatproof grease.

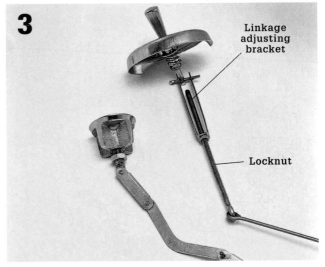

3

- Linkage adjusting bracket
- Locknut

Adjust the pop-up stopper mechanism by first loosening the locknut on the lift rod. If the stopper doesn't close all the way, shorten the linkage by screwing the rod ⅛" farther into the linkage-adjusting bracket. If the stopper doesn't open wide enough, extend the linkage by unscrewing the rod ⅛". Tighten the locknut before replacing the mechanism and testing your adjustment.

16. Unclogging Sink Drains

Every sink has a drain trap and a fixture drain line. Sink clogs usually are caused by a buildup of soap and hair in the trap or fixture drain line. Remove clogs by using a plunger, disconnecting and cleaning the trap, or using a hand auger.

Many sinks hold water with a mechanical plug called a pop-up stopper. If the sink will not hold standing water, or if water in the sink drains too slowly, the pop-up stopper must be cleaned and adjusted.

Tools & Materials ▸

Plunger
Channel-type pliers
Small wire brush
Screwdriver
Flashlight

Rag
Bucket
Replacement gaskets
Teflon tape

Clogged lavatory sinks can be cleared with a plunger (not to be confused with a flanged force-cup). Remove the pop-up drain plug and strainer first, and plug the overflow hole by stuffing a wet rag into it, allowing you to create air pressure with the plunger.

How to Clear a Sink Trap

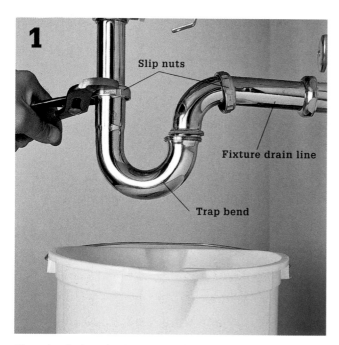

1

Slip nuts

Fixture drain line

Trap bend

Place bucket under trap to catch water and debris. Loosen slip nuts on trap bend with channel-type pliers. Unscrew nuts by hand and slide away from connections. Pull off trap bend.

2

Dump out debris. Clean trap bend with a small wire brush. Inspect slip nut washers for wear, and replace if necessary. Reinstall trap bend and tighten slip nuts.

How to Clear a Kitchen Sink

Plunging a kitchen sink is not difficult, but you need to create an uninterrupted pressure lock between the plunger and the clog. If you have a dishwasher, the drain tube needs to be clamped shut and sealed off at the disposer or drainline. The pads on the clamp should be large enough to flatten the tube across its full diameter (or you can clamp the tube ends between small boards).

If there is a second basin, have a helper hold a basket strainer plug in its drain or put a large pot or bucket full of water on top of it. Unfold the skirt within the plunger and place this in the drain of the sink you are plunging. There should be enough water in the sink to cover the plunger head. Plunge rhythmically for six repetitions with increasing vigor, pulling up hard on the last repitition. Repeat this sequence until the clog is removed. Flush out a cleared clog with plenty of hot water.

How to Use a Hand Auger at the Trap Arm

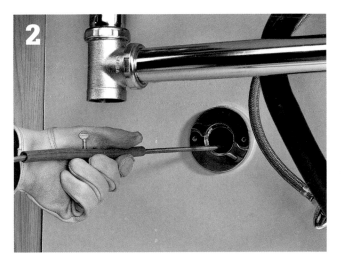

If plunging doesn't work, remove the trap and clean it out (see previous page). With the trap off, see if water flows freely from both sinks (if you have two). Sometimes clogs will lodge in the T-fitting or one of the waste pipes feeding it. These may be pulled out manually or cleared with a bottlebrush or wire. When reassembling the trap, apply Teflon tape clockwise to the male threads of metal waste pieces. Tighten with your channel-type pliers. Plastic pieces need no tape and should be hand tightened only.

If you suspect the clog is downstream of the trap, remove the trap arm from the fitting at the wall. Look in the fixture drain with a flashlight. If you see water, that means the fixture drain is plugged. Clear it with a hand auger (see page 63).

17. Clearing Main Drains

If using a plunger or a hand auger does not clear a clog in a fixture drain line, it means that the blockage may be in a branch line, the main waste-vent stack, or the sewer service line.

First, use an auger to clear the branch drain line closest to any stopped-up fixtures. Branch drain lines may be serviced through the cleanout fittings located at the end of the branch. Because waste water may be backed up in the drain lines, always open a cleanout with caution. Place a bucket and rags under the opening to catch waste water. Never position yourself directly under a cleanout opening while unscrewing the plug or cover.

If using an auger on the branch line does not solve the problem, then the clog may be located in a main waste-vent stack. To clear the stack, run an auger cable down through the roof vent. Make sure that the cable of your auger is long enough to reach down the entire length of the stack. If it is not, you may want to rent or borrow another auger. Always use extreme caution when working on a ladder or on a roof.

If no clog is present in the main stack, the problem may be located in the sewer service line. Locate the main cleanout, usually a Y-shaped fitting at the bottom of the main waste-vent stack. Remove the plug and push the cable of a hand auger into the opening.

Some sewer service lines in older homes have a house trap. The house trap is a U-shaped fitting located at the point where the sewer line exits the house. Most of the fitting will be beneath the floor surface, but it can be identified by its two openings. Use a hand auger to clean a house trap.

If the auger meets solid resistance in the sewer line, retrieve the cable and inspect the bit. Fine, hair-like roots on the bit indicate the line is clogged with tree roots. Dirt on the bit indicates a collapsed line.

Use a power auger to clear sewer service lines that are clogged with tree roots. Power augers (page 74 to 75) are available at rental centers. However, a power auger is a large, heavy piece of equipment. Before renting, consider the cost of rental and the level of your do-it-yourself skills versus the price of a professional sewer cleaning service. If you rent a power auger, ask the rental dealer for complete instructions on how to operate the equipment.

Always consult a professional sewer cleaning service if you suspect a collapsed line.

Tools & Materials ▸

Adjustable wrench or pipe wrench	Penetrating oil
Hand auger	Cleanout plug (if needed)
Cold chisel	Pipe joint compound
Ball-peen hammer	Electrical drum auger
Bucket	Gloves
Ladder	Teflon Tape
Phillips screwdriver	
Rags	

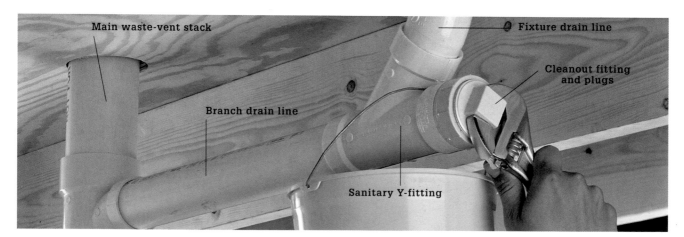

Clear a branch drain line by locating the cleanout fitting at the end of the line. Place a bucket underneath the opening to catch waste water, then slowly unscrew the cleanout plug with an adjustable wrench. Clear clogs in the branch drain line with a hand auger.

How to Clear a Branch Drain Line

Clear the main waste and vent stack by running the cable of a hand auger down through the roof vent. Always use extreme caution while working on a ladder or roof.

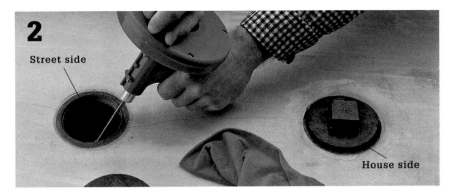

Clear the house trap in a sewer service line using a hand auger. Slowly remove only the plug on the "street side" of the trap. If water seeps out the opening as the plug is removed, the clog is in the sewer line beyond the trap. If no water seeps out, auger the trap. If no clog is present in the trap, replace the street-side plug and remove the house-side plug. Use the auger to clear clogs located between the house trap and main stack.

How to Replace a Main Drain Cleanout Plug

Remove the cleanout plug, using a large wrench. If the plug does not turn out, apply penetrating oil around the edge of the plug, wait 10 minutes, and try again. Place rags and a bucket under fitting opening to catch any water that may be backed up in the line.

Remove stubborn plugs by placing the cutting edge of a cold chisel on the edge of the plug. Strike the chisel with a ball-peen hammer to move plug counterclockwise. If the plug does not turn out, break it into pieces with the chisel and hammer. Remove all broken pieces.

Replace the old plug with a new plug. Apply pipe joint compound to the threads of the replacement plug and screw into the cleanout fitting.

Alternate: Replace the old plug with an expandable rubber plug. A wing nut squeezes the rubber core between two metal plates. The rubber bulges slightly to create a watertight seal.

How to Power-Auger a Floor Drain

Remove the cover from the floor drain using a slotted or Phillips screwdriver. On one wall of the drain bowl you'll see a cleanout plug. Remove the cleanout plug from the drain bowl with your largest channel-type pliers. This cleanout allows you to bypass the trap. If it's stuck, apply penetrating oil to the threads and let it sit a half an hour before trying to free it again. If the wrench won't free it, rent a large pipe wrench from your home center or hardware store. You can also auger through the trap if you have to.

Power Auger Large Lines ▸

If you choose to auger a larger line, you may find yourself opening a cleanout with 10 or 20 vertical feet of waste water behind it. Be careful. The cap may unexpectedly burst open when it's loose enough, spewing noxious waste water uncontrollably over anything in its path, including you! Here are some precautions:

Whenever possible, remove a trap or cleanout close to the top of the backed-up water level. Run your auger through this. Make sure the auger and its electric connections will not get wet should waste water spew forcefully from the cleanout opening.

Use the spear tool on the power auger first, to let the water drain out through a smaller hole before widening it with a larger cutting tool. If you are augering through a 3 or 4" cleanout, use three bits: the spear, a small cutter, and then a larger cutter to do the best job.

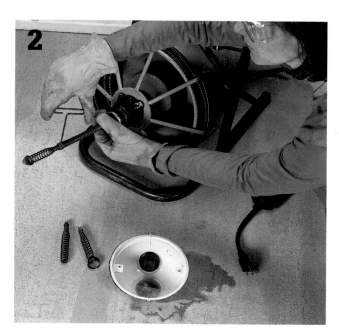

Rent an electric drum auger with at least 50 feet of ½-inch cable. The rental company should provide a properly sized, grounded extension cord, heavy leather gloves, and eye protection. The auger should come with a spear tool, cutter tool, and possibly a spring tool suitable for a 2-inch drainline. Attach the spearhead first (with the machine unplugged).

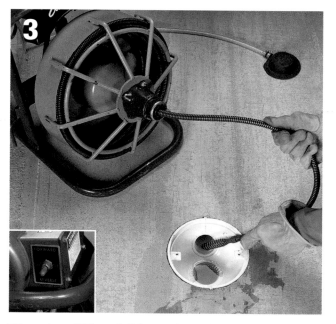

Wear close-fitting clothing and contain long hair. Place the power auger machine in a dry location within 3 ft. of the drain opening. Plug the tool into a grounded, GFI-protected circuit. Wear eye protection and gloves. Position the footswitch where it is easy to actuate. Make sure the FOR/REV switch is in the Forward position (inset photo). Hand feed the cleaning tool and some cable into the drain or cleanout before turning the machine on.

Stationary power augers (as opposed to pistol-grip types) are controlled by a foot pedal called an actuator so you can turn the power on and off hands-free.

With both gloved hands on the cable, depress the foot actuator to start the machine. Gradually push the rotating cable into the drain opening. If the rotation slows or you cannot feed more cable into the drain, pull back on the cable before pushing it forward again. Don't force it. The cable needs to be rotating whenever the motor is running or it can kink and buckle. If the cleaning tool becomes stuck, reverse it, back the tool off the obstruction, and switch back to Forward.

Gradually work through the clog by pulling back on the cable whenever the machine starts to bog down and push it forward again when it gains new momentum. Never let the cable stop turning when the motor is running. When you have broken through the clog or snagged an object, withdraw the cable from the line. Manually pull the cable from the drain line while continuing to run the drum Forward. When the cleaning tool is close to the drain opening, release the foot actuator and let the cable come to a stop before feeding the last 2 or 3 ft. of cable into the drum by hand.

After clearing the drain pipe, run the auger through the trap. Finish cleaning the auger. Wrap Teflon tape clockwise onto the plug threads and replace the plug. Run hot water through a hose from the laundry sink or use a bucket to flush remaining debris through the trap and down the line.

18. Replacing a Kitchen Sink

Most drop-in, self-rimming kitchen sinks are easily installed.

Drop-in sinks for do-it-yourself installation are made from cast iron coated with enamel, stainless steel, enameled steel, acrylic, fiberglass, or resin composites. Because cast-iron sinks are heavy, their weight holds them in place and they require no mounting hardware. Except for the heavy lifting, they are easy to install. Stainless steel and enameled-steel sinks weigh less than cast-iron and most require mounting brackets on the underside of the countertop. Some acrylic and resin sinks rely on silicone caulk to hold them in place.

If you are replacing a sink, but not the countertop, make sure the new sink is the same size or larger. All old silicone caulk residue must be removed with acetone or denatured alcohol, or else the new caulk will not stick.

Tools & Materials ▸

Caulk gun	Plumber's putty
Spud wrench	or silicone caulk
Screwdriver	Mounting clips
Sink	Jigsaw
Sink frame	Pen or pencil

Shopping Tips ▸

- When purchasing a sink, you also need to buy strainer bodies and baskets, sink clips, and a drain trap kit.
- Look for basin dividers that are lower than the sink rim—this reduces splashing.
- Drain holes in the back or to the side make for more usable space under the sink.
- When choosing a sink, make sure the predrilled openings will fit your faucet.

Drop-in sinks, also known as self-rimming sinks, have a wide sink flange that extends beyond the edges of the sink cutout. They also have a wide back flange to which the faucet is mounted directly.

How to Install a Self-Rimming Sink

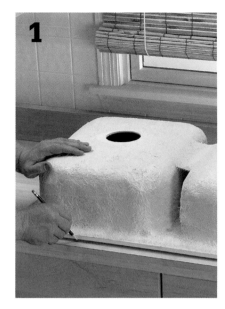

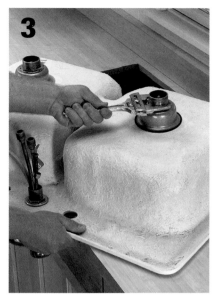

Invert the sink and trace around the edges as a reference for making the sink cutout cutting lines, which should be parallel to the outlines, but about 1" inside of them to create a 1" ledge. If your sink comes with a template for the cutout, use it.

Drill a starter hole and cut out the sink opening with a jigsaw. Cut right up to the line. Because the sink flange fits over the edges of the cutout, the opening doesn't need to be perfect, but as always you should try to do a nice, neat job.

Attach as much of the plumbing as makes sense to install prior to setting the sink into the opening. Having access to the underside of the flange is a great help when it comes to attaching the faucet body, sprayer, and strainer, in particular.

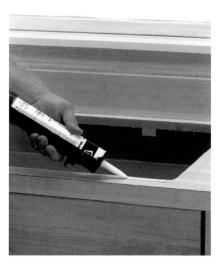

Apply a bead of silicone caulk around the edges of the sink opening. The sink flange most likely is not flat, so try and apply the caulk in the area that will make contact with the flange.

Place the sink in the opening. Try to get the sink centered right away so you don't need to move it around and disturb the caulk, which can break the seal. If you are installing a heavy cast-iron sink, it's best to leave the strainers off so you can grab onto the sink at the drain openings.

For sinks with mounting clips, tighten the clips from below using a screwdriver or wrench (depending on the type of clip your sink has). There should be at least three clips on every side. Don't overtighten the clips—this can cause the sink flange to flatten or become warped.

19. Replacing a Kitchen Faucet

Most new kitchen faucets feature single-handle control levers and washerless designs that rarely require maintenance. Additional features include brushed metallic finishes, detachable spray nozzles, or even push-button controls.

Connect the faucet to hot and cold water lines with easy-to-install flexible supply tubes made from vinyl or braided steel. If your faucet has a separate sprayer, install the sprayer first. Pull the sprayer hose through the sink opening and attach to the faucet body before installing the faucet.

Where local codes allow, use plastic tubes for drain hookups. A wide selection of extensions and angle fittings lets you easily plumb any sink configuration. Manufacturers offer kits that contain all the fittings needed for attaching a food disposer or dishwasher to the sink drain system.

Tools & Materials ▸

Adjustable wrench	Scouring pad
Basin wrench or	Scouring cleaner
channel-type pliers	Plumber's putty
Hacksaw	Flexible vinyl or
Faucet	braided steel
Putty knife	supply tubes
Screwdriver	Drain components
Silicone caulk	Penetrating oil

Modern kitchen faucets tend to be single-handle models, often with useful features such as a pull-out head that functions as a sprayer. This Price Pfister™ model comes with an optional mounting plate that conceals sink holes when mounted on a predrilled sink flange.

Choosing a New Kitchen Faucet

You'll find many options when choosing a new kitchen faucet. The best place to start the process is with your sink. In the past, most faucets were mounted directly to the sink deck, which had three or four predrilled holes to accommodate the faucets, spout, sprayer, and perhaps a liquid soap dispenser or an air gap for your dishwasher. Modern kitchen faucets don't always conform to this setup, with many of them designed to be installed in a single hole in the sink deck or in the countertop. If you plan to keep your old sink, look for a faucet that won't leave empty holes in the deck. Generally, it's best to replace like for like, but unfilled stainless sink holes can be filled with snap-in plugs or a soap dispenser.

The two most basic kitchen faucet categories are single-handle and two-handle. Single-handle models are much more popular now because you can adjust the water temperature easily with just one hand.

Another difference is in the faucet body. Some faucets have the taps and the spout mounted onto a faucet body so the spacing between the tailpieces is preset. Others, called widespread faucets, have independent taps and spouts that can be configured however you please, as long as the tubes connecting the taps to the spouts reach. This type is best if you are installing the faucet in the countertop (a common way to go about it with new countertops such as solid surface, quartz, or granite).

In the past, kitchen faucets almost always had a remote pull-out sprayer. The sprayer was attached to the faucet body with a hose directly below the mixing valve. While this type of sprayer is still fairly common, many faucets today have an integral pull-out spout that is very convenient and less prone to failure than the old-style sprayers.

A single-handle, high arc faucet with traditional remote sprayer. The mounting plate is decorative and optional.

Single-handle faucets may require four holes, as does this model with its side sprayer and matching soap/lotion dispenser.

Two-handled faucets are less common, but remain popular choices for traditional kitchens. The gooseneck spout also has a certain elegance, but avoid this type if you have a shallow sink that's less than 8" deep.

A single-handle faucet with pull-out spray head requires only one hole in your sink deck or countertop—a real benefit if your sink is not predrilled or if it is an undermount model.

How to Remove an Old Faucet

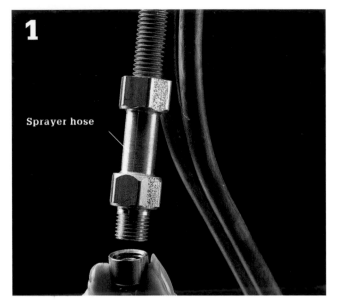

To remove the old faucet, start by clearing out the cabinet under the sink and laying down towels. Turn off the hot and cold stop valves and open the faucet to make sure the water is off. Detach the sprayer hose from the faucet sprayer nipple and unscrew the retaining nut that secures the sprayer base to the sink deck. Pull the sprayer hose out through the sink deck opening.

Spray the mounting nuts that hold the faucet or faucet handles (on the underside of the sink deck) with penetrating oil for easier removal. Let the oil soak in for a few minutes.

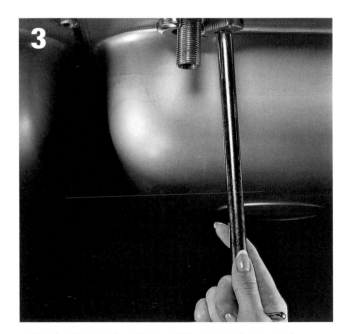

Unhook the supply tubes at the stop valves. Don't reuse old chrome supply tubes. If the stops are missing or unworkable, replace them. Then remove the coupling nuts and the mounting nuts on the tailpieces of the faucet with a basin wrench or channel-type pliers.

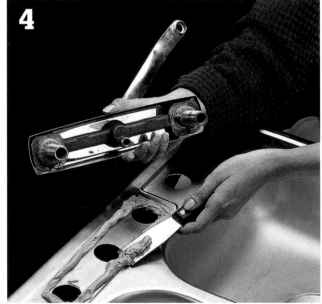

Pull the faucet body from the sink. Remove the sprayer base if you wish to replace it. Scrape off old putty or caulk with a putty knife and clean off the sink with a scouring pad and an acidic scouring cleaner like Bar Keeper's Friend®. *Tip: Scour stainless steel with a back and forth motion to avoid leaving unsightly circular markings.*

How to Install a Kitchen Sink Faucet

Shut off hot and cold water at the faucet stop valves.
Assemble the parts of the deck plate that cover the outer mounting holes in your sink deck (unless you are installing a two-handle faucet, or mounting the faucet directly to the countertop, as in an undermount sink situation). Add a ring of plumber's putty in the groove on the underside of the base plate.

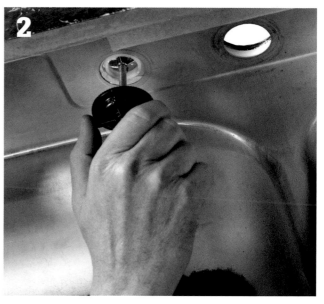

Set the base plate onto the sink flange so it is correctly aligned with the predrilled holes in the flange. From below, tighten the wing nuts that secure the deck plate to the sink deck.

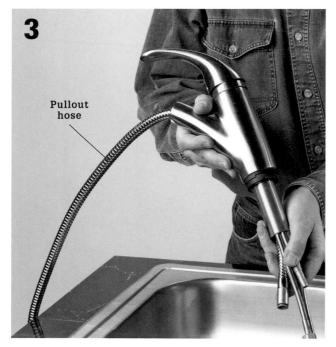

Retract the pullout hose by drawing it out through the faucet body until the fitting at the end of the hose is flush with the bottom of the threaded faucet shank. Insert the shank and the supply tubes down through the top of the deck plate.

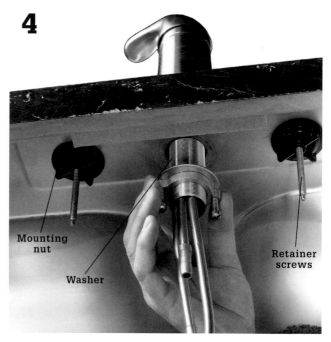

Slip the mounting nut and washer over the free ends of the supply tubes and pullout hose, then thread the nut onto the threaded faucet shank. Hand tighten. Tighten the retainer screws with a screwdriver to secure the faucet.

(continued)

Slide the hose weight onto the pullout hose (the weight helps keep the hose from tangling and it makes it easier to retract).

Connect the end of the pullout tube to the outlet port on the faucet body using a quick connector fitting.

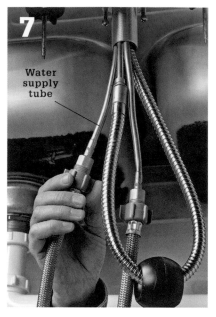

Water supply tube

Hook up the water supply tubes to the faucet inlets. Make sure the lines are long enough to reach the supply risers without stretching or kinking.

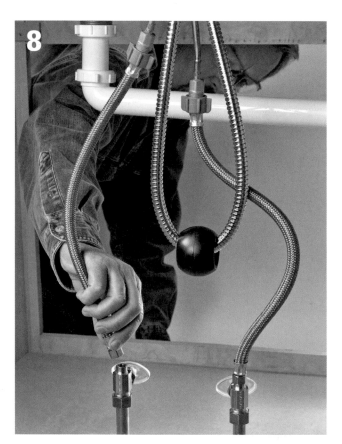

Connect the supply lines to the supply risers at the stop valves. Make sure to get the hot lines and cold lines attached correctly.

Attach the spray head to the end of the pullout hose and turn the fitting to secure the connection. Turn on water supply and test. *Tip: Remove the aerator in the tip of the spray head and run hot and cold water to flush out any debris.*

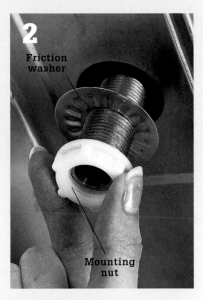

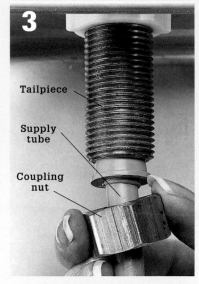

Apply a thick bead of silicone caulk to the underside of the faucet base and then insert the tailpieces of the faucet through the appropriate holes in the sink deck. Press down lightly on the faucet to set it in the caulk.

Slip a friction washer onto each tailpiece and then hand tighten a mounting nut. Tighten the mounting nut with channel-type pliers or a basin wrench. Wipe up any silicone squeeze-out on the sink deck with a wet rag before it sets up.

Connect supply tubes to the faucet tailpieces. Make sure the tubes you buy are long enough to reach the stop valves and that the coupling nuts will fit the tubes and tailpieces.

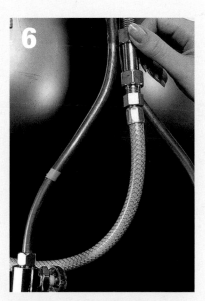

Apply a ¼" bead of plumber's putty or silicone caulk to the underside of the sprayer base. With the base threaded onto the sprayer hose, insert the tailpiece of the sprayer through the opening in the sink deck.

From beneath, slip the friction washer over the sprayer tailpiece and then screw the mounting nut onto the tailpiece. Tighten with channel-type pliers or a basin wrench. Wipe any excess putty or caulk on the sink deck from around the base.

Screw the sprayer hose onto the hose nipple on the bottom of the faucet. Hand tighten and then give the nut one quarter turn with channel-type pliers or a basin wrench. Turn on the water supply at the shutoff, remove the aerator, and flush debris from the faucet.

20. Connecting a Kitchen Drain

Kitchen sink drains don't last forever, but on the plus side, they're very easy and inexpensive to replace. The most common models today are made of PVC plastic pipe and fittings held together with slip fittings. In addition to making the installation fairly forgiving, the slip fitting makes the drain easy to disassemble if you get a clog. The project shown here is a bit unusual by today's standards, in that it does not include either a dishwasher drain or a garbage disposer. But you will see how to add each of these drain systems to your kitchen sink in the following two chapters.

You can buy the parts for the kitchen drain individually (you can usually get better quality materials this way) or in a kit (see photo, next page). Because most kitchen sinks have two bowls, the kits include parts for plumbing both drains into a shared

trap, often with a baffle in the T-fitting where the outlet line joins with the tailpiece from the other bowl. If you are installing a disposer, consider installing individual traps to eliminate the baffle, which reduces the flow capacity by half.

Tools & Materials ▸

Flat screwdriver
Spud wrench
Trap arm
Mineral spirits
Cloth
Strainer kit
Plumber's putty

Teflon tape
Washers
Waste-T fitting
S- or P-trap

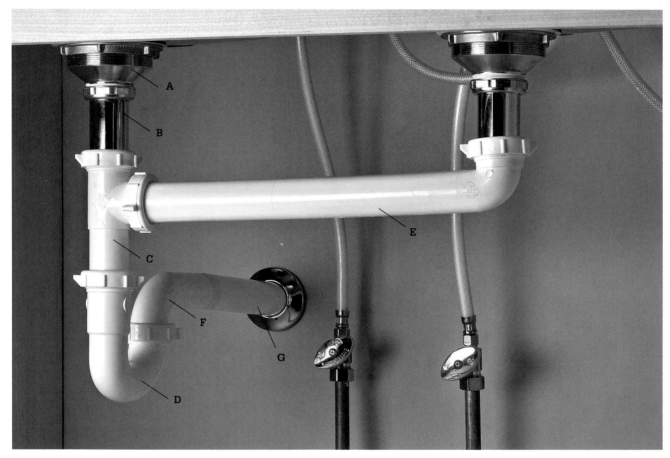

Kitchen sink drains include a strainer basket (A), tailpiece (B), continuous waste T (C), P- or S-trap (D), outlet drain lines (E), trap arm (F), and wall stubout (G).

Drain Kits ▸

Kits for installing a new sink drain include all the pipes, slip fittings, and washers you'll need to get from the sink tailpieces (most kits are equipped for a double bowl kitchen sink) to the trap arm that enters the wall or floor. For wall trap arms, you'll need a kit with a P-trap. For floor drains. you'll need an S-trap. Both drains normally are plumbed to share a trap. Chromed brass or PVC with slip fittings let you adjust the drain more easily and pull it apart and then reassemble if there is a clog. Kitchen sink drains and traps should be 1½" o.d. pipe—the 1¼" pipe is for lavatories and doesn't have enough capacity for a kitchen sink.

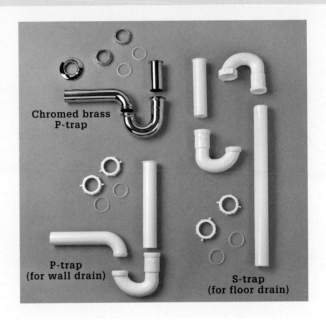

Chromed brass
P-trap

P-trap
(for wall drain)

S-trap
(for floor drain)

Tips for Choosing Drains ▸

Wall thickness varies in sink drain pipes. The thinner plastic material is cheaper and more difficult to obtain a good seal with the thicker, more expensive tubing. The thin product is best reserved for lavatory drains, which are far less demanding.

Slip joints are formed by tightening a male-threaded slip nut over a female-threaded fitting, trapping and compressing a beveled nylon washer to seal the joint.

Use a spud wrench to tighten the strainer body against the underside of the sink bowl. Normally, the strainer flange has a layer of plumber's putty to seal beneath it above the sink drain, and a pair of washers (one rubber, one fibrous) to seal below.

How to Connect a Kitchen Sink Drain

If you are replacing the sink strainer body, remove the old one and clean the top and bottom of the sink deck around the drain opening with mineral spirits. Attach the drain tailpiece to the threaded outlet of the strainer body, inserting a nonbeveled washer between the parts if your strainer kits include one. Lubricate the threads or apply Teflon tape so you can get a good, snug fit.

Apply plumber's putty around the perimeter of the drain opening and seat the strainer assembly into it. Add washers below as directed and tighten the strainer locknut with a spud wrench (see photo, previous page) or by striking the mounting nubs at the top of the body with a flat screwdriver.

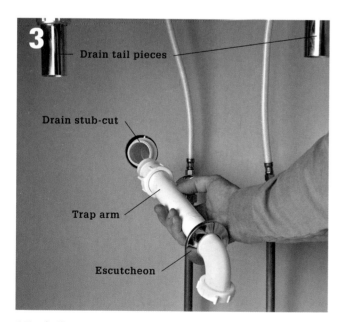

Drain tail pieces

Drain stub-cut

Trap arm

Escutcheon

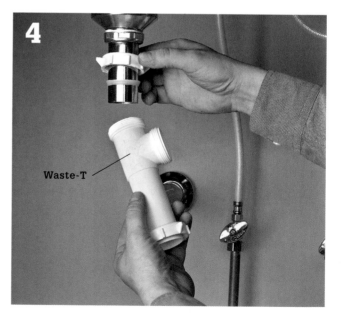

Waste-T

Attach the trap arm to the male-threaded drain stubout in the wall, using a slip nut and beveled compression washer. The outlet for the trap arm should point downward. *Note: The trap arm must be higher on the wall than any of the horizontal lines in the set-up, including lines to dishwasher, disposer, or the outlet line to the second sink bowl.*

Attach a waste-T-fitting to the drain tailpiece, orienting the opening in the fitting side so it will accept the outlet drain line from the other sink bowl. If the waste-T is higher than the top of the trap arm, remove it and trim the drain tailpiece.

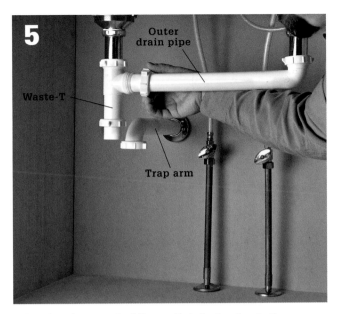

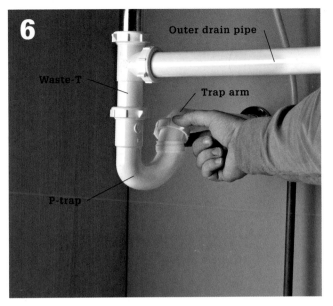

Joint the short end of the outlet drain pipe to the tailpiece for the other sink bowl and then attach the end of the long run to the opening in the waste-T. The outlet tube should extend into the T ½" or so—make sure it does not extend in far enough to block water flow from above.

Attach the long leg of a P-trap to the waste-T and attach the shorter leg to the downward-facing opening of the trap arm. Adjust as necessary and test all joints to make sure they are still tight, and then test the system.

Variation: Drain in Floor ▸

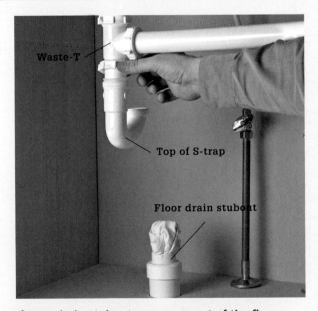

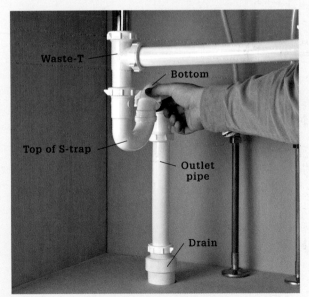

If your drain stubout comes up out of the floor instead of the wall, you'll need an S-trap to tie into it instead of a P-trap. Attach one half of the S-trap to the threaded bottom of the waste-T.

Attach the other half of the S-trap to the stubout with a slip fitting. This should result in the new fitting facing downward. Join the halves of the S-trap together with a slip nut, trimming the unthreaded end if necessary.

21. Patching Burst Pipes

If a water pipe freezes and breaks, your first priority may be getting it working again—whatever it takes. There are a number of temporary fix products out there, some involving clamps and sleeves, others, epoxy putties and fiberglass tape. These repairs usually can get you through a weekend okay. We also show you how to apply full slip repair couplings, a more permanent fix. Whatever repair approach you take, please, please, please, don't leave for the store without first determining a) the diameter of your pipe and b) the material of your pipe.

Tools & Materials ▸

Metal file
Repair clamps
Marker
Tubing cutter
Adjustable wrench
Pliers

Water supply pipes can burst for many reasons, but the most common cause is water freezing and expanding inside the pipe. First turn off the water, then apply a fix.

How to Patch Pipes with Repair Clamps

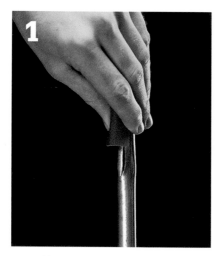

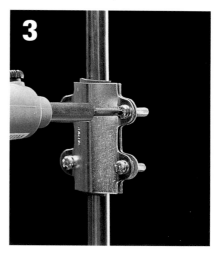

Dry off the damaged area of the pipe and file down any sharp edges with a metal file. Place the rubber sleeve that comes with the repair clamp around the ruptured area. The seam should be on the opposite side of the pipe from the damage.

Position the two halves of the repair clamp so the rubber sleeve is sandwiched between the repair clamps.

Insert bolts through the bolt holes in the repair clamp and thread nuts onto the ends. Tighten the bolts until the pressure from the clamp seals the damages area. *Note: This is a temporary repair only. Replace the damaged pipe as soon as possible.*

How to Install a Repair Coupling

For a longer lasting (not permanent) repair, use a compression-fit, full-slip repair coupling. These come with parts to make a compression union—you can also buy a slip coupling that's just a piece of copper tubing with an inside diameter equal to the outside diameter of the tubing being repaired, but these require soldering. Turn off water at the nearest control valve. Mark the boundaries of the pipe section to be replaced.

Full slip repair coupling

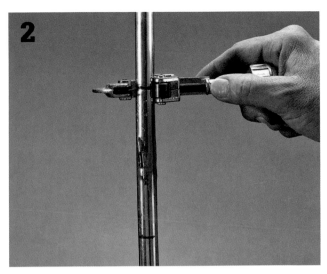

Cut out the damaged pipe section with a tubing cutter. Both wheels of the cutter should rest evenly on the pipe. Rotate the cutter around the pipe. The line it cuts should make a perfect ring, not a spiral. Tighten the cutter a little with each rotation until the pipe snaps. Repeat at your other mark.

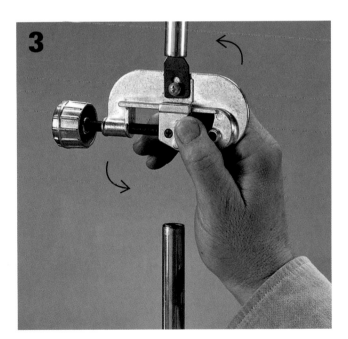

Deburr the insides of the pipes with the triangular blade on the tubing cutter.

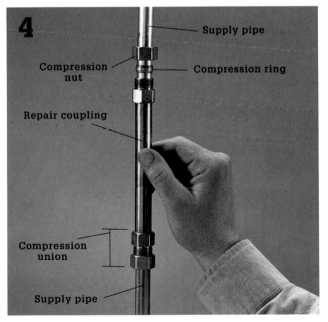

Supply pipe
Compression nut
Compression ring
Repair coupling
Compression union
Supply pipe

Slip the compression nuts and rings supplied with the repair coupling onto the cut ends of the pipe being repaired and then slip the repair coupling over one end. Slide the coupling farther onto the pipe and then slide it back the other way so it fits over the other pipe section and the repair area is centered inside the coupling. Tighten each compression nut with pliers while stabilizing the coupling with an adjustable wrench.

22. Installing Shutoff Valves

Worn-out shutoff valves or supply tubes can cause water to leak underneath a sink or other fixture. First, try tightening the fittings with an adjustable wrench. If this does not fix the leak, replace the shutoff valves and supply tubes.

Shutoff valves are available in several fitting types. For copper pipes, valves with compression-type fittings are easiest to install. For plastic pipes, use grip-type valves. For galvanized iron pipes, use valves with female threads.

Older plumbing systems often were installed without fixture shutoff valves. When repairing or replacing plumbing fixtures, you may want to install shutoff valves if they are not already present.

Tools & Materials ▸

Hacksaw
Tubing cutter
Adjustable wrench
Tubing bender

Felt-tipped pen
Shutoff valves
Supply tubes
Pipe joint compound

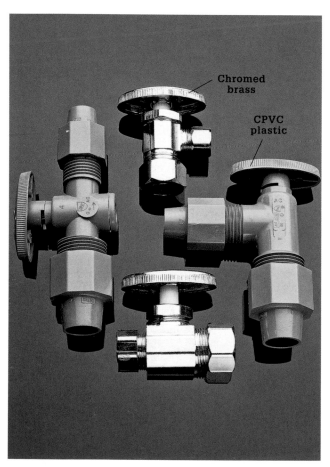

Shutoff valves allow you to shut off the water to an individual fixture so it can be repaired. They can be made from durable chromed brass or lightweight plastic. Shutoff valves come in ½" and ¾" diameters to match common water pipe sizes.

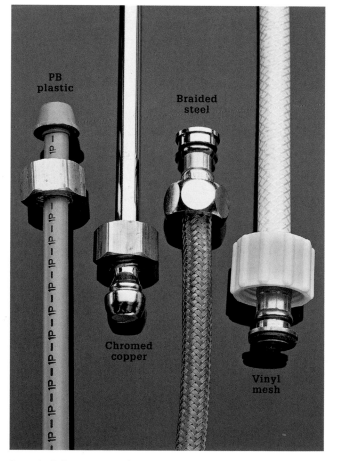

Supply tubes are used to connect water pipes to faucets, toilets, and other fixtures. They come in 12", 20", and 30" lengths. PB plastic and chromed copper tubes are inexpensive. Braided steel and vinyl mesh supply tubes are easy to install.

How to Install Shutoff Valves & Supply Tubes

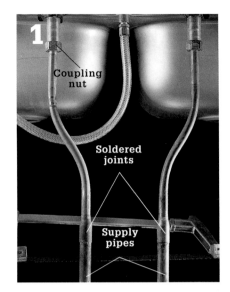

Turn off water at the main shutoff valve. Remove old supply pipes. If pipes are soldered copper, cut them off just below the soldered joint, using a hacksaw or tubing cutter. Make sure the cuts are straight. Unscrew the coupling nuts and discard the old pipes.

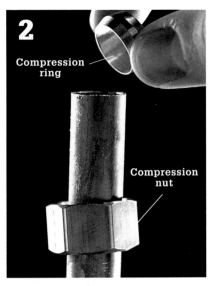

Slide a compression nut and a compression ring over the copper water pipe. Threads of the nut should face the end of the pipe.

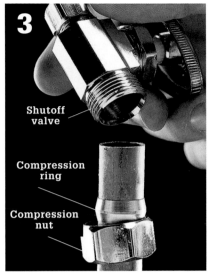

Apply pipe joint compound to the threads of the shutoff valve or compression nut. Screw the compression nut onto the shutoff valve and tighten with an adjustable wrench.

Bend chromed copper supply tube to reach from the tailpiece of the fixture to the shutoff valve, using a tubing bender. Bend the tube slowly to avoid kinking the metal.

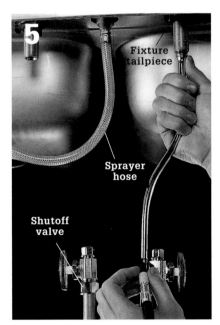

Position the supply tube between fixture tailpiece and the shutoff valve, and mark the tube to length. Cut the supply tube with a tubing cutter.

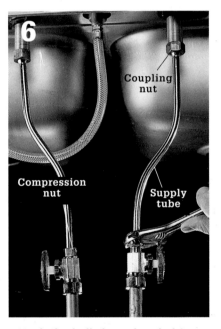

Attach the bell-shaped end of the supply tube to the fixture tailpiece with a coupling nut, then attach the other end to the shutoff valve with compression ring and nut. Tighten all fittings with an adjustable wrench.

APPENDIX: Plumbing Tools

Many plumbing projects and repairs can be completed with basic hand tools you probably already own. Adding a few simple plumbing tools will prepare you for all the projects in this book. Specialty tools, such as a snap cutter or appliance dolly, are available at rental centers. When buying tools, invest in quality products.

Always care for tools properly. Clean tools after using them, wiping them free of dirt and dust with a soft rag. Prevent rust on metal tools by wiping them with a rag dipped in household oil. If a metal tool gets wet, dry it immediately, and then wipe it with an oiled rag. Keep toolboxes and cabinets organized. Make sure all tools are stored securely.

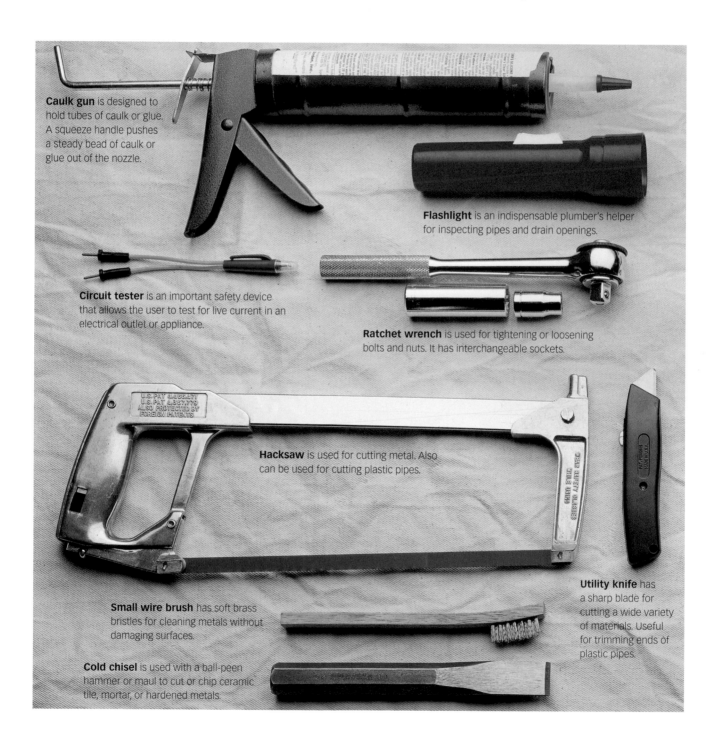

Caulk gun is designed to hold tubes of caulk or glue. A squeeze handle pushes a steady bead of caulk or glue out of the nozzle.

Flashlight is an indispensable plumber's helper for inspecting pipes and drain openings.

Circuit tester is an important safety device that allows the user to test for live current in an electrical outlet or appliance.

Ratchet wrench is used for tightening or loosening bolts and nuts. It has interchangeable sockets.

Hacksaw is used for cutting metal. Also can be used for cutting plastic pipes.

Utility knife has a sharp blade for cutting a wide variety of materials. Useful for trimming ends of plastic pipes.

Small wire brush has soft brass bristles for cleaning metals without damaging surfaces.

Cold chisel is used with a ball-peen hammer or maul to cut or chip ceramic tile, mortar, or hardened metals.

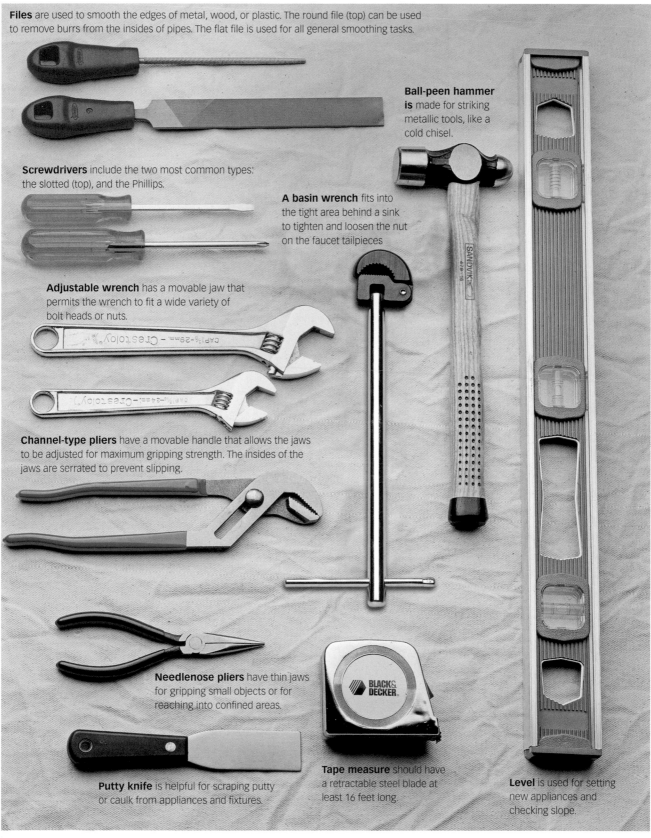

Files are used to smooth the edges of metal, wood, or plastic. The round file (top) can be used to remove burrs from the insides of pipes. The flat file is used for all general smoothing tasks.

Ball-peen hammer is made for striking metallic tools, like a cold chisel.

Screwdrivers include the two most common types: the slotted (top), and the Phillips.

A basin wrench fits into the tight area behind a sink to tighten and loosen the nut on the faucet tailpieces

Adjustable wrench has a movable jaw that permits the wrench to fit a wide variety of bolt heads or nuts.

Channel-type pliers have a movable handle that allows the jaws to be adjusted for maximum gripping strength. The insides of the jaws are serrated to prevent slipping.

Needlenose pliers have thin jaws for gripping small objects or for reaching into confined areas.

Putty knife is helpful for scraping putty or caulk from appliances and fixtures.

Tape measure should have a retractable steel blade at least 16 feet long.

Level is used for setting new appliances and checking slope.

(continued)

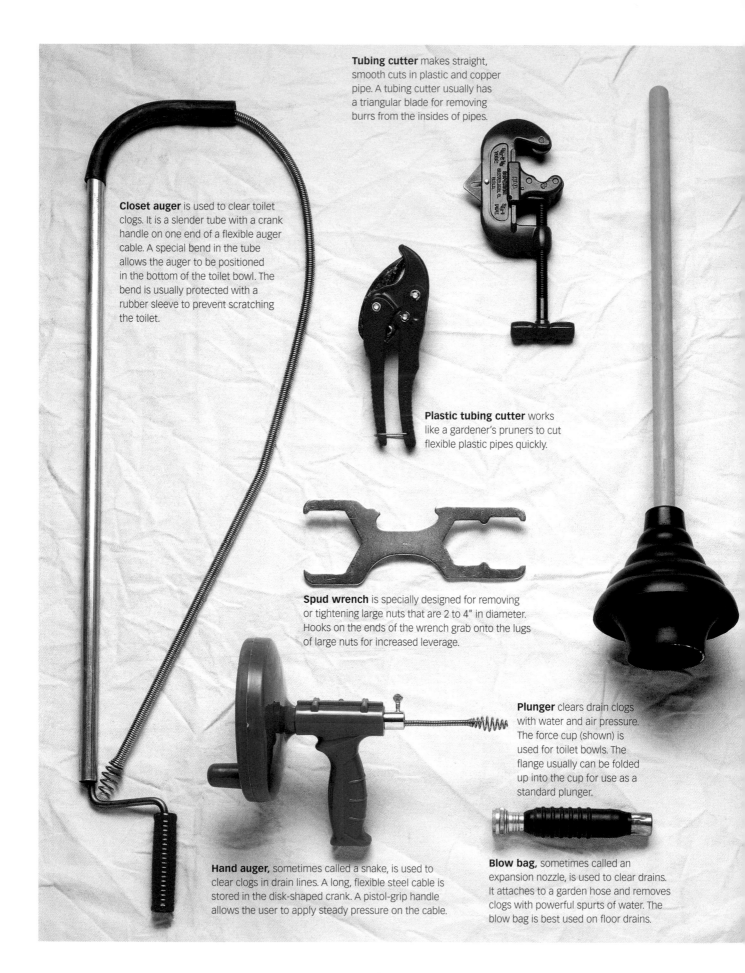

Tubing cutter makes straight, smooth cuts in plastic and copper pipe. A tubing cutter usually has a triangular blade for removing burrs from the insides of pipes.

Closet auger is used to clear toilet clogs. It is a slender tube with a crank handle on one end of a flexible auger cable. A special bend in the tube allows the auger to be positioned in the bottom of the toilet bowl. The bend is usually protected with a rubber sleeve to prevent scratching the toilet.

Plastic tubing cutter works like a gardener's pruners to cut flexible plastic pipes quickly.

Spud wrench is specially designed for removing or tightening large nuts that are 2 to 4" in diameter. Hooks on the ends of the wrench grab onto the lugs of large nuts for increased leverage.

Plunger clears drain clogs with water and air pressure. The force cup (shown) is used for toilet bowls. The flange usually can be folded up into the cup for use as a standard plunger.

Hand auger, sometimes called a snake, is used to clear clogs in drain lines. A long, flexible steel cable is stored in the disk-shaped crank. A pistol-grip handle allows the user to apply steady pressure on the cable.

Blow bag, sometimes called an expansion nozzle, is used to clear drains. It attaches to a garden hose and removes clogs with powerful spurts of water. The blow bag is best used on floor drains.

Propane torch (left) is used for soldering fittings to copper pipes. Light the torch quickly and safely using a spark lighter (above).

Pipe wrench has a movable jaw that adjusts to fit a variety of pipe diameters. Pipe wrench is used for tightening and loosening pipes, pipe fittings, and large nuts. Two pipe wrenches often are used together to prevent damage to pipes and fittings.

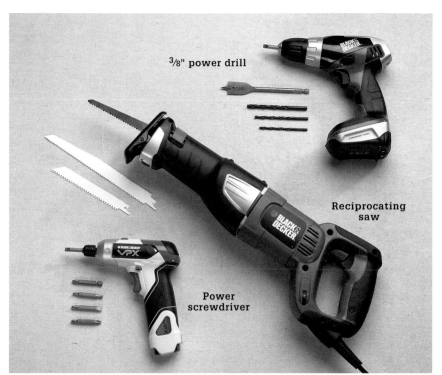

³⁄₈" power drill

Reciprocating saw

Power screwdriver

Power hand tools can make any job faster, easier, and safer. Cordless power tools offer added convenience. Use a cordless ³⁄₈" power drill for virtually any drilling task.

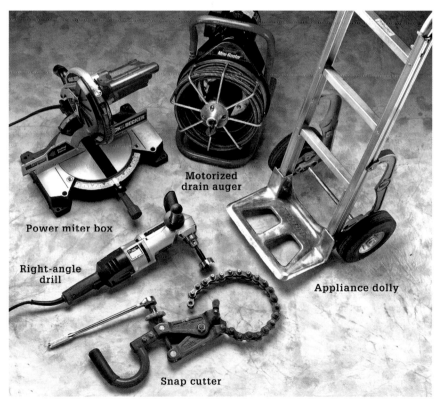

Motorized drain auger

Power miter box

Right-angle drill

Appliance dolly

Snap cutter

Rental tools may be needed for large jobs and special situations. A power miter saw makes fast, accurate cuts in a wide variety of materials, including plastic pipes. A motorized drain auger clears tree roots from sewer service lines. Use an appliance dolly to move heavy objects like water heaters. A snap cutter is designed to cut tough cast-iron pipes. The right-angle drill is useful for drilling holes in hard-to-reach areas.

Creative Publishing international

Copyright © 2010
Creative Publishing international, Inc.
400 First Avenue North, Suite 300
Minneapolis, Minnesota 55401
1-800-328-0590
www.creativepub.com

Printed at R.R. Donnelley

10 9 8 7 6 5 4 3 2 1

Here's How Plumbing
Created by: The Editors of Creative Publishing international, Inc., in cooperation with Black & Decker. Black & Decker® is a trademark of The Black & Decker Corporation and is used under license.

President/CEO: Ken Fund
VP for Sales & Marketing: Kevin Hamric

Home Improvement Group

Publisher: Bryan Trandem
Managing Editor: Tracy Stanley
Senior Editor: Mark Johanson
Editor: Jennifer Gehlhar

Creative Director: Michele Lanci-Altomare
Senior Design Managers: Jon Simpson, Brad Springer
Design Manager: James Kegley

Lead Photographer: Joel Schnell

Production Managers: Linda Halls, Laura Hokkanen

Page Layout Artist: Danielle Smith